Twayne's United States Authors Series

Sylvia E. Bowman, *Editor*

INDIANA UNIVERSITY

George Ade

GEORGE ADE

by LEE COYLE

John Carroll University

 63

Twayne Publishers, Inc.   ::   New York

FOR
BETTY, MARLEE AND SUZY

Preface

ON A LECTURE TOUR to America in 1915, Sir Walter Raleigh, the English man of letters, fell into conversation with a professional orator. They talked of American literature. In a letter to his wife, Raleigh wrote: "The orator screamed with delight when I said that George Ade is the greatest living American writer. 'O, tell them that at Brown' he said, 'tell them that at Brown! If you, coming as an Oxford professor, tell them that at Brown, I don't know what'll happen!' "*

In 1915 the consternation at Brown would have been spontaneous and spectacular; but, if today one were to announce George Ade as a great American writer, he would get a dazed look and the slightly delayed question, "George *Who?*"

Those who are aware that George Ade existed are usually familiar with his work as a fabulist, but rarely as a playwright, though half of his most productive years were devoted to the theater. Many of Ade's plays are unpublished, some have been lost, and virtually all have been forgotten. In this study I have drawn liberally on Ade's published and unpublished plays and have devoted considerable space to the first substantial survey of this neglected aspect of his career.

George Ade's popularity at the turn of the century and for a decade beyond was enormous, but his fame is now gone: his books are out of print, and his readers rare. While I do not think it will ever be otherwise, Ade's accomplishment and stature as a minor American author deserve examination.

Ade is not complex, and infrequently is he deep. What he wrote was simple, clear, and direct; consequently, I have subordinated analysis to exposition and comment in this first, full-length assessment of the work of George Ade. In it, I have felt free to illustrate at length from Ade's works, especially from his unpublished plays; but I have also quoted freely from his published works, for they are either rare or not readily accessible to the average reader.

* *Letters of Sir Walter Raleigh,* I, 416.

Among the many persons and institutions who have contributed to the making of this small book are Professors George E. Grauel, Warren Fleischauer, Lyon N. Richardson, and Arthur F. White. George Ade Davis, Ade's nephew and heir, has been patient with my questions and generous with his permission to quote from Ade's published and unpublished work. I am also indebted to Fred C. Kelly, Ade's biographer, and to the library staffs of Western Reserve University, John Carroll University, the Indiana Historical Society, the Chicago Historical Society, the State Library of Massachusetts, New York Public Library, Cleveland Public Library, and the Library of Congress.

It is a pleasure to thank Editor Sylvia E. Bowman for her precise and painstaking help, and I must also thank the Bobbs-Merrill Company for giving me special permission to reprint quotations from *George Ade: Warmhearted Satirist*.

Tradition places the typist last in the acknowledgments. I beg my wife's pardon for the injustice.

LEE COYLE

John Carroll University
October, 1963

Contents

Chronology

1866   George Ade born February 9 in Kentland, Indiana: the fifth child of John and Adaline Ade. As a youth, he attended the village schools.

1881   October, Ade's first work, "A Basket of Potatoes," appeared in the Kentland *Gazette*.

1883   September, entered Purdue University. He served briefly as an editor of *Purdue*, the only student publication; he contributed frequently to this monthly periodical.

1887   With seven others Ade graduated from Purdue. His commencement oration: "The Future of Letters in the West."

1888   Became a reporter on the Lafayette *Morning News*, a short-lived Republican party organ. He soon moved to the Lafayette *Call*, an evening paper.

1890   In Chicago he joined the staff of the *Morning News*, later known as the *News-Record* and finally the *News*.

1893   November 20, Ade began a new department in the *Record* called "Stories of the Streets and of the Town."

1896   Published *Artie*.

1897   September 1, Ade published his first fable in slang. Earlier that year *Pink Marsh* appeared.

1898   Traveled extensively in southern and eastern Europe.

1899   *Doc' Horne* and *Fables in Slang*.

1900   *More Fables*. On September 30 Ade's first syndicated fable appeared. Traveled in China and Japan. In the following years he made many trips to Europe.

1901   *Forty Modern Fables*.

1902   *The Girl Proposition*. Ade's first musical, *The Sultan of Sulu*, opens on Broadway.

1903   *Peggy from Paris*, *People You Know*, and *In Babel*.

1904   *Breaking into Society* and *True Bills*. Three plays produced on Broadway: *The Sho-Gun, The College Widow,* and *The County Chairman.*

1905   *Just Out of College* and *The Bad Samaritan.* Traveled to Egypt.

1906   *In Pastures New.*

1907   *Artie,* a dramatic adaptation of his first book.

1908   *Father and the Boys.*

1909   *The Fair Coed.*

1910   *The Old Town.*

1912   *Knocking the Neighbors.*

1914   *Ade's Fables.*

1918   Published *Marse Covington,* a one-act play written in 1906. Ade wrote a number of one-acters among which are *Nettie, The Mayor and the Manicure,* and *Speaking to Father.*

1920   *Hand-made Fables.*

1922   *Single Blessedness and Other Observations.*

1926   Honorary L.H.D. from Purdue University. A year later he was granted an honorary L.L.D. from Indiana University.

1928   *Bang! Bang!*

1931   *The Old-Time Saloon.*

1941   *Stories of the Streets and of the Town.*

1944   May 16, died at Brook, Indiana.

George Ade

CHAPTER *1*

Cockleburs and Corn

> Once there was an undersized Town that
> had the Corn-Fields sneaking up on all sides
> of it, trying to break over the Corporation
> Line. People approaching the Town from the
> North could not see it, because there was a
> Row of Willow-Trees in the Way.
>
> —"The Fable of the Red-Letter
> Night at Smartweed Junction."

BORN FEBRUARY 9, 1866, of middle-class parents, George
Ade opened his eyes in Kentland, Indiana, a typical northwestern Hoosier community tucked away in the cornbelt four
miles from the border of Illinois. While George was aborning,
townsmen, some in blue army overcoats, inquired about his
arrival while doing business at the Discount & Deposit Bank
where the infant's father was cashier. The boy was John Ade's
fifth child and third son. He and his wife Adaline had lost
an infant daughter, but on the whole the Lord was good to
them; and they were God-fearing people, substantial, respected,
hard-working.

The new child was a full-fledged Hoosier, but his parents
were not. His father was an emigree from England; his mother,
from Ohio. For six years they had lived in Kentland, watching
the town burgeon until their new son had 599 fellow humans
to inquire after his health.

I *Boyhood*

Ade's simple home faced the village square, but its back-
yard was the prairie with its magic wastes, its animals, birds,
wild flowers, blackberry thickets, and cattail-rimmed sloughs.

Chiggers and mosquitoes abounded, and a boy measured his adventures with lumpy arms and legs.

Slowly the cornfields elbowed their way into the prairie lands; and, as the boy lengthened, they deepened and spread. The abundant corn was fuel for the hungry sheet-iron stoves that sparred with winter like paunchy boxers. It was less expensive than wood and cheaper to burn than to store. The boy never forgot the huge, rock-hard, golden ears of corn darting into the rumbling flames.

The town was as exciting as the prairie, for it was as complete as a thousand other small American towns: it had twice as many saloons as churches, a drugstore, a newspaper office, a livery stable, a clothing store, a watchmaker, and a general store. Kentland entered the Gilded Age proudly, and although Ade recalled that its architecture ran to cubes and its landscaping was designed by Ute Indians, it welcomed the missionaries of culture. A traveling troupe brought *Ten Nights in a Bar-Room* and *Lady Audley's Secret* to Kentland; other festivities included panoramic lectures on the Holy Land, Swiss bell-ringers, revival meetings, the circus, traveling medicine shows, and lady elocutionists who recited "Rum's Maniac" with chilling intensity and who froze blood with "Curfew Shall Not Ring Tonight."

There was home-grown culture, too: the harmonica, jew's-harp, melodeon, guitar, and the ubiquitous male quartet. E. P. Roe was the novelist of the hour, and sheet music sold by the ton. Then the cardboard motto came along: "Before the women began running yarn through cardboard, every front room had been a sarcophagus gleaming with cold horsehair and bearing on the walls doleful reminders, in crayon, of the kinsfolk who had passed on. Now the dim sanctuary began to brighten up with preserved leaves which had been sprinkled with diamond-dust and 'God Bless Our Home' done in mottled colors."[1]

Temperance crusades were popular in Kentland as elsewhere, and Ade wore a blue ribbon that entitled him to hate bottled beer with the vehemence usually reserved for whiskey. Every boy aspired to own a gold toothpick, a cigar-holder, a watch, and a watch-chain made of human hair. And rare was the Hoosier who did not lust to see "Iolanthe, the Sleeping Beauty," done in butter at the Interstate Exposition in Chicago.

Along the wooden sidewalks of Kentland strutted the harbingers of high fashion, and the boy was dazzled by hoopskirts, bustles, pill-box hats, twirling parasols, fluttering fans, and pert chignons. He envied the dandies their slick, shiny hair and artful ringlets; their spring-bottom trousers; gates-ajar collars; pillow-like cravats; box-toed boots; and narrow-rimmed, high-crowned derbies "lined with puckery silk, and resembling, according to Abe Martin, the interior of a child's coffin."[2]

The American school everywhere was dominated by Mc-Guffey's Readers, and rural schools had the additional spice of "assifidity" bags worn next to the skin where body heat ripened the odor. The assafetida may not have warded off the measles, but the scholar with the bag was rarely jostled by society.

For a healthy child, life was bright and wholesome, simple and gay in Kentland in the 1870's. There were rabbit hunting and ice skating, enormous meals to eat, corn to pop and nuts to crack, and occasionally an oyster supper held at McCullough's Hall. There was usually a drunk in the town jail, and there were also political rallies to attend, tall talk to grin at, Christmas trees to trim, and in the summer a picket fence to walk on or a hammock to swing in.

If a boy were lucky, he had an odd job that brought in a little cash. George got twenty-five cents a month from the marshal for lighting the lamp on his block. Each evening at dusk he took a pocketful of brimstone matches, climbed a ladder, and coaxed the charred wick of a coal-oil burner to catch fire. The lamp gave off a thin, sad, flickering light that merely authenticated the surrounding darkness, but it paid.

One of Ade's most vivid boyhood memories was mud: "My surest recollections of the 'seventies in northwestern Indiana is that for weeks and months we were held prisoner by the mud. We might as well have been surrounded by blank prison walls."[3] The roads became impassable after a moderate rainfall, for the rich, black soil of Indiana turned into an oozy muck from one to two feet deep, that made transportation impossible except by horseback.

During the winter months, when the joys of freedom on the prairie marked time, there were books, magazines, and newspapers for the boy to read. There was talk of politics, too. Grant had disposed of Greeley, who died broken-hearted three weeks after the general's re-election; but Republicans in Indiana and elsewhere were suffering exquisitely from exposures of corruption in the Grant administration. The political fireworks were gorgeous, for it was the era of yellow journalism when editors were loaded with canisters of invective and editorials discharged vituperation rather than logic. Instead of "my worthy opponent," orators of the period roared "that filthy scoundrel. . . ." Local politics were discussed in terms understandable to an adolescent.

Ade's youthful Republicanism inspired him to at least one adventure in the no man's land of political morality. In the campaign of 1878 during the Hayes administration, the boy sidled into the offices of the Democratic organ and borrowed a batch of proof sheets that hung on the wall. With his heart pounding joyously at the theft, he bolted for Republican headquarters where his resourcefulness and diligence in the cause of right were applauded. The purloined proofs contained the Democrats' final attack before the election. To add to the twelve-year-old boy's estimation of his political coup was a public denunciation of the "infamous skunk" who stole the proof sheets. The Democratic editor declared that "never again must the air of our sanctum be contaminated by the fumes emanating from his filthy carcass."[4] Things like that make life worth-while.

Dime novels were the comic-books of the nineteenth century and the boy read his share on the sly. A few of the titles available at the time were *The Shadow Scout! or, Screaming Moses of the Fishkill Mountains; Thayendanegea, The Scourge or, The War-Eagle of the Mohawks: A Tale of Mystery, Ruth, and Wrong; Merciless Ben, the Hair Lifter;* and *The Death-Mystery: A Crimson Tale of Life in New York.* But Mark Twain and Charles Dickens could be read openly, and Ade read about Huck Finn, Tom Sawyer, David Copperfield, and Martin Chuzzlewit under the approving eyes of his parents.

An avid reader and a close observer of life in his community, the boy found that it was not difficult to put thoughts on paper. And his teacher soon discovered that the gangling scholar with the sharply chiseled features had a rare talent for expression. Ade's facile pen dashed off compositions that earned him the reputation of being a bright, promising lad. In his early teens he wrote a paper entitled "A Basket of Potatoes" which his teacher promptly sent to the editor of the Kentland *Gazette* for publication.

"A Basket of Potatoes" is a tightly written, conventional essay on life. Its subject has a grand sweep; its tone is cocksure;

but in its economy of expression may be seen the tender shoots of Ade's mature style. The last paragraph of the essay is a fair sample of the whole:

> Life is but a basket of potatoes. When the hard jolts come, the big will rise and the small will fall. The true, the honest and the brave will go to the top. The small-minded and ignorant must go to the bottom. And now I would like to say something to these young potatoes. Now is the time for you to say whether or not in the battle of life you will be a small or large potato. If you would be a large potato get education, be honest, observing and careful and you will be jolted to the top. If you would be a small potato neglect these things and you will get to the bottom of your own accord. Break off your bad habits, keep away from rotten potatoes and you will get to the top. Be careless of these things and you will reach the bottom in due time. Everything rests with you. Prepare for the jolting.[5]

"Of course, when I wrote about those potatoes," commented Ade in later years, "I didn't know that there were so many rutabagas, turnips and yams mixed up with the other vegetables."[6]

All in all, Ade's boyhood was serene. His parents were kindly and understanding, his community was comfortable, his schooling adequate, his environment friendly. The townsfolk considered him a healthy, bright, young whippersnapper; but they had temporary reservations about his father's mentality when he decided to send the boy to college. And, anyway, who ever heard of Purdue?

II *On Chauncey Hill*

John Ade's decison to send his son to college was based more on desperation than conviction. He had sired a lad who lived in the heart of a farming community but hated farming. He preferred cockleburs to corn, hated horses, detested working with his hands, and believed that most farmers were brutalized by their labor.

George learned about farmwork the hard way. His parents imposed few restrictions on their children; but, believing that idle hands tempted the devil, they insisted that George work on a farm during his summer vacations from high school. "I did not volunteer," he wrote. "I was drafted. My parents thought that if they kept me away from the gaieties and temptations of a village of eight hundred people I might grow up to be a good citizen."[7]

He worked long, hard hours—and bitterly hated every moment of his slavery. To Ade, farm life was sordid, depressing, and destructive of man's feelings for beauty. He remembered threshing time and the "thirty or forty men and ten million flies, all reporting for dinner." The farmer joined his help at table, caught sight of a vase of flowers that his wife had placed there, and snarled: "Can we eat them things? Take 'em away."[8]

The Newton County superintendent of schools visited John Ade one day and offered a solution to his problem: send George to college. All reports indicated that the boy should refine his natural gifts. John Ade was not a man to shy away from difficult ideas or hard decisions. He talked with a number of friends and associates, all of whom shook their heads and said college was a waste of four years and a thousand dollars. John Ade was undisturbed by the criticism that Purdue would waste four years of George's life. He suspected that George would probably manage that by staying at home, but he was troubled about the money. Hardly a parsimonious man, John Ade was conversely a victim of Christian generosity and an uncanny knack of pressing money on precisely the people most unable to repay it. He researched the problem carefully, and he discovered that the commissioners of each Indiana county had the right to grant two scholarships each year to a state college. The only requirement: a good moral character. George was in. Application for a scholarship from Newton County was made and granted immediately: no one else had applied.

Ade was ready to enter the ten-year-old college dedicated to the agricultural and mechanical arts, but his mother refused to launch a sixteen-year-old boy into the world. The temptations of Lafayette, a town of fifteen thousand, would surely prove his damnation. Although he had finished the two-year high school course in Kentland, Ade took post-graduate courses for another year to harden his soul against the seductions of Lafayette.

In the fall of 1883 he traveled the fifty long miles between Kentland and Lafayette, and then he took his first long walk from the railroad station to the tiny college on Chauncey Hill. He was impressed by the pathetic scattering of brick buildings and vowed that he would uphold all of Purdue's fine traditions. Years later, after having been a trustee of Purdue, he recalled his undergraduate days and his ignorance of Purdue's limitations at that time:

> Let me tell you what we *didn't* have. No fraternity or club houses. No Athletic Association and no teams of any kind playing inter-collegiate schedules. No glee-club. No dramatic club. No band. No daily paper—just a puny magazine that came out once a month. No annual book until 1889 when John McCutcheon nagged his class into getting out the first "debris." No stadium, no ceremonials, no dress parades. Maybe I can indicate a synopsis of our absolute yappiness by telling you that in the whole dormitory the only suit of evening cloths was owned by Shrewsbury Beauregard Miller of Charleston, West Virginia, and when he arrayed himself and started for the city to attend a "hop" we of the submerged class would lean out of our windows and hoot at him.[9]

Ade entered fully into college life: he joined the Irving Literary Society, which sniped at the rival Carlyle Literary Society; went on picnics on the banks of the Wabash and returned home in the moonlight singing "Upidee"; was generally attentive to his studies, but slighted physics and zoology; wrote and recited on "Education by Contact," "The Abolitionist as a Type," "Leaders," and "Popular Fallacies." Rising to all occasions, he learned the schottische, the Newport, waltzes, quadrilles, Virginia reels, and polkas, equaling therein his mastery of physics and zoology.

Popular among his twenty-nine fellow freshmen (the entire student body numbered two hundred) Ade was also well known at the box office of the Grand Opera House in Lafayette. The dramatic fare was exceptional for a small town, for troupes traveling between Cincinnati and Chicago took respite in Lafayette and made the evening pay. Ade, who seldom missed a show, first saw in Lafayette Nat Goodwin, Edwin Booth, Helena Modjeska, and the famous minstrelmen, George Thatcher, Willis P. Sweatnam, Billy Rice, and Lew Docksteder. There, too, he saw the Hoyt farces, the light operas *La Mascotte, Nanon, Girofle-Girofla,* and *Olivette*. Most important of all, *The Mikado* came to Lafayette during his junior year and exposed him to what became a life-long attack of Gilbert and Sullivan.

Ade discovered other delights at Purdue: Sweet Caporal and Richmond Straight Cut cigarettes; Sigma Chi Fraternity; the *Purdue,* a monthly literary periodical which he edited for a semester; a co-ed named Lillian Howård; and an under-classman, John Tinney McCutcheon, to whom he took a liking. McCutcheon, who became one of Ade's closest friends, wrote of him during their college days:

> He was thin and tall and wore a sedate blue suit with tight spring-bottomed trousers that flared out at the ankle. And he had three outstanding characteristics which made him an inviting subject for caricature: an unusual expanse of head behind the ears, a sweep of strongly marked eyebrows and a striking lack of abdominal fullness, described by realists as slab belly.[10]

Ade's record at Purdue was not brilliant. He enjoyed the humanities and suffered from the sciences; he wrote a few literary papers that were remarkable only for their conversational style. But college was infinitely better than farm work; and, though it seemed a toss-up between mathematics and manual labor, someone always helped him with his math. A big man on a small campus, he was much in demand for his wit, his genius for observation, and his willingness to drop everything to dash in to Lafayette or to Indianapolis to see a show.

By the time Ade graduated in June, 1887, he had lost most of his shyness and had a certificate of release from working in the fields. After all, a Sigma Chi who delivered a commencement oration on "The Future of Letters in the West" couldn't be expected to bale hay.

CHAPTER *2*

Rutabagas, Turnips, and Yams

When he was still a Young Man he made the Important Discovery that the honest Laborer who digs Post-Holes for 11 hours at a Stretch gets $1.25 in the Currency of the Realm, while the Brain-Worker who leads out a Spavined Horse and puts in 20 minutes at tall Bunko Work, can clean up $14.50 and then sit on the Porch all Afternoon, reading "The Lives of the Saints."

—"Self-Made Hezekiah and His Message of Hope to This Year's Crop of Graduates."

ADE LEFT PURDUE clutching his degree in one hand and filling an empty pocket with the other. His father and the Kentland Skeptical Society were looking at him out of the corners of their eyes; so with an indifferent heart he yielded to social pressure and declared for the law.

I *Lafayette*

Back in Lafayette, George read Blackstone in a law office near the Grand Opera House. After his first day he clearly saw that he was up against a kind of verbal mathematics that made a punching bag of his brain; but he stuck it out for almost two months. He was still on the dole from his father, and his only qualification for employment, beyond his degree from Purdue, was an aversion to farm work. Fortunately something turned up.

A group of Lafayette Republicans decided to start a political newspaper that could be used as a howitzer in the presidential campaign of 1888. George applied for a job and was hired as the paper's only reporter; his salary: eight dollars a week, a sum occasionally paid. The *Morning Call* was the answer that Ade had been seeking: he was happy in a job that paid a salary, even if intermittent, for observing human relationships. Writing was no chore, politics was fun, and he hadn't yet had his fill of Lafayette. He was content.

Unfortunately the *Morning Call* had financial laryngitis. For three weeks he went without pay and was put off with vague promises about a raise. "Payday was approaching," he wrote, "and the funds had dribbled away, the backers had fled, the editor-in-chief had evaporated, the editorial writer had gone to Delphi to see his girl, the business manager was in retirement, the city editor had flown to Crawfordsville." The paper's only reporter and the composing room foreman were left to pull the shroud over the dead journal, "so cold and calm, and purged of political hatreds."[1]

George bounced into another reporting job within a few days of the *Morning Call's* demise. This time he reported for the Lafayette *Call*, an evening paper that paid two dollars a week less than his former job, but his salary came regularly. Of course he sometimes received meal tickets, as part of his pay, honored at a beanery that advertised; but Fridays now produced something more substantial than promises.

While working on the *Call*, Ade became friendly with George Barr McCutcheon, a reporter on the rival evening paper, the *Courier*. McCutcheon was the brother of John T., Ade's fraternity brother at Purdue. Both were fond of the theater, particularly of the minstrels; and they became close friends.

Journalism satisfied Ade completely, but he was seduced by a patent medicine company in Lafayette that offered to double his salary. Writing advertisements and promoting a popular patent medicine made from a secret, pleasant, and popular combination of rye whiskey, syrup, and bitters, offered Ade few challenges; but he managed to serve all America by minting a slogan for a laxative his firm was manufacturing in the interests of profit and national regularity: Cascarets. Throughout the United States worried people were assured that "They work while you sleep." Ade got a three-dollar raise.

Life was sweet and bright for Ade. He was the pet of Lafayette, sought after, widely known. He had plenty of time to read and loaf, and he continued to take an interest in matters on Chauncey Hill. In fact, George might have settled permanently

in Lafayette, except for a rapid chain of events that sent him
flying to Chicago. He had fallen in love with Lillian Howard, a
senior at Purdue; but he had failed to make the grade with Miss
Howard's mother, a female tartar who was worked up over
the world's spiritual welfare. Mrs. Howard couldn't get a clean
shot at the world, so she directed her fire at the most vul-
nerable target handy. Religion was not a popular subject with
Ade, but he found himself running down the track head-on
into a Methodist locomotive.[2] For a while he avoided the
Howard's front porch, and in his absence a Baptist minister
backed into the roundhouse and crowded him onto a siding.
Lillian married the minister and went to live in Minnesota.
Shortly thereafter the patent medicine company suffered a
change in management and the King of Cascarets was eliminated
from the payroll.

For several months Ade had been receiving importunate
letters from John T. McCutcheon who had joined the art department of the Chicago *Morning News.* Ade wasn't particularly
interested in going to Chicago, but a quick tally of his assets
advised the swift purchase of a train ticket to somewhere.

Twenty-four-years-old, penniless, jobless, in debt to the sis-
ters Niemansverdriet who operated his boardinghouse in Lafayette, and half-frightened of being dumped into the bustling
vigor of Chicago, George Ade saw nothing gay about June, 1890.

II *Chicago Sacked*

Ade arrived in Chicago with "a suitcase which looked like
leather, which it was not, and a very small trunk which looked
like pressed paper, which it was."[3] To himself he was a country
Jake short on what it took to make good in a big city. Fortunately John T. McCutcheon had persuaded Charles Dennis, the
city editor of the *Morning News,* to give Ade an interview.
McCutcheon touted Ade highly.

Dennis liked the gangling youth and hired him at twelve
dollars a week. Ade's first assignment was a daily piece on the
weather. He developed a passion for the subject. He interviewed
bell hops, bank presidents, policemen, meteorologists, teamsters,
and dozens of perspiring citizens about their reaction to a heat
wave. He quickly developed an appetite for Chicago and de-
voured the city with his senses. "After I went on the morning
News for a tryout," he wrote, "I had small confidence in my

ability. I was afraid of the cable cars and my own shadow. I had only one asset which helped to shove me forward from the start . . . *I was interested in all kinds of people and what they were doing and hoping to do.*"[4]

Ade became a familiar face at the theaters, ball parks, prize fights, lectures, and beer gardens. He adopted Chicago—a sprawling, dirty, rough-neck town full of brass knuckles, loud laughter, easy money, and exquisite suffering. Gambling houses, brothels, pool halls, and saloons boomed and multiplied. The levee district was unsafe after dark, and the morgue registered several new guests every day. Streetwalkers, pickpockets, cutthroats, tramps, and country cousins who didn't make the grade infested the night with their poison. But there was a brawny, wholesome Chicago, too, for many of the city's million people were newcomers: Norwegians, Poles, Swedes, Danes, Croatians, Bohemians, Greeks, Lithuanians, and Germans. Immigrants by the thousand streamed into Chicago and doubled its population in the decade before 1890. Ade knew them before the melting began.

Having won his spurs on the paper, Ade moved up to general assignments that ranged from covering strikes to attending *Schutzenfests*. From court trials, charity balls, and city council meetings, he observed and listened and wrote. He covered sporting events, sermons, inquests, parades, murders, disasters, and conventions. At first hand, he saw Chicago's crudeness and gentility, its filth and its virtues. From the red-light district to the Columbian Exposition, Chicago was his; and the cornbelt was a million miles away.

Fully as important as Chicago in Ade's development were his fellow newspapermen. If he found stimulation in the streets, he found inspiration at the office and at the Whitechapel Club of which he was a member. Among his friends were Brand Whitlock, Ray Stannard Baker, Peter Finley Dunne, Opie Read, Eugene Field, Kirke La Shelle, James O'Donnell Bennett, Frank Vanderlip, John Hertz, and the artists Charlie Williams and Carl Emil Schultze, the creator of "Foxy Grandpa." During the 1890's Ade became friendly with many actors and actresses, including Joseph Jefferson, Henry Irving, Otis Skinner, Minnie Maddern Fiske, and William H. Crane; he met Hamlin Garland, Lillian Russell, John L. Sullivan, Colonel Robert G. Ingersoll, and other personalities of the day.

The 1890's have become the golden age of American reminiscence, and Americans today look back with a grin to a decade
jaunty with the Gibson Girl, the free lunch, Mr. Dooley, the
nickel beer, the bicycle built for two, John Philip Sousa, Gentleman Jim Corbett, Buffalo Bill, "Sweet Rosie O'Grady," and the
glories of the Barbary Coast. It was all that—and far more.
This decade valued William Dean Howells but read Mark
Twain; watched the sad progress of Coxey's army as it marched
on Washington; it beheld the garrotting of old ways and the
glamorizing of new. Politics and class strife frequently wrecked
the peace, the revolt from the village began, and intellectual
war was declared upon academic authority and upon traditional
values. It was also the decade that witnessed the immense popularity of Edward Bellamy's Utopian novel, *Looking Backward*
(1888), which gave rise to the "Nationalist movement" and
impetus to the agrarian protest which gave birth to the Populist
party.

Moreover, this decade turned its back on the problems born
of the Civil War to solve new problems spawned by machines,
factories, and raw ideas. The Sherman Anti-Trust Law was
enacted; the Pullman Strike brought Federal troops to Chicago;
Eugene Debs was jailed. There were Boss Croker, Mark Hanna,
and John Peter Altgeld, the Cross of Gold, and the Lizzie Borden
case; also, the 1890's suffered the panic of '93, the foreshadowing
of prohibition in the rant of the Anti-Saloon League, and at
the end of the decade San Juan Hill and then Aguinaldo and
the Philippine Insurrection. Not all was quaint and charming.
There is a shot of bitters in the schooner of nostalgia.

The big guns of literature were Howells, Twain, and James
in America; Hardy, Kipling, and Conrad in England. But Ade
was little influenced by the literary giants of his day. He lusted
after the fame and fortune of the Eugene Fields, Arthur Bris-
banes, and Finley Peter Dunnes that he and all America knew.

Ade's enthusiasms were for people, journalism, financial success, good talk, and good times. Later in life he added golf. He
was not particularly interested in national affairs, social problems,
intellectual achievement, ideas, the arts, culture, religion, or
technological advancements. He was a youth with a ukelele; and
life was to be one grand, sweet, happy song. He never changed,
and he got what he wanted from life. The riches came; the
talk was good; and the good times were many.

In Chicago, Ade was an active member of the Whitechapel Club,

a little group of thirsty intellectuals who were opposed to every-thing. The fact that Jack the Ripper was their patron saint will give a dim idea of the hard-boiledness of the organization. They had kind words and excuses for many of the anarchists who had been hanged for the bomb-throwing at the Haymarket riot. They were social revolutionists and single-taxers and haters of the rich. They scoffed at the conventional and orthodox and deplored the cheap futility of their own slave-tasks as contributors to the daily press. They were young men enjoying their first revolt.[5]

The principal activities of the club were talking, smoking, drinking, and scorning commercialism. It was not unusual for the police to come and testify to the success of the club's ac-tivities. And everybody in Chicago remembered Club Member Collins.

Collins was a penniless intellectual who loved the poor and hated everybody who wasn't starving. His theory was that America needed martyrs to awaken the national conscience to the horrors of capitalist exploitation. Collins proposed that the members organize a mass suicide to pound home the lesson. He argued eloquently that dramatically planned suicides for a high purpose would be both effective and satisfying. While expatiating on his gory plan, one of the Whitechapel members suggested that he kick-off the festivities. Collins greeted the suggestion with enthusiasm and agreed to be first if the others wouldn't think it pushy.

With a vote of confidence Collins returned to his shabby hotel room on Clark Street and downed a tankard of poison. He died slowly and passed the time writing an impassioned account of his immediate sensations and the more universal pains of mankind. He bade farewell to all and asked that the Whitechapel members collect his remains and cremate them "on account of" he was broke.

The membership approved Collins' last request and took what was left of him to Miller's Station, Indiana, on the shore of Lake Michigan. There they built a funeral pyre, drenched it with coal oil, capped it with Collins, made a few speeches before touching it off, and then went in swimming until the ashes cooled enough for them to gather up the martyr's charred rem-nants. Collins' skull and a few odds and ends were put in a flour sack and brought back to the club rooms. Everyone conceded that Collins was a great guy with "lousy" ideas.[6]

About a decade later at the height of his success as a playwright, Ade's zest for good fellowship, gaiety, and collegiate pranks was unabated. One of his favorite diversions while in New York City was to hire a hack, drive down Eighth Avenue with Booth Tarkington, and pirate canteloupes and watermelons from the sidewalk stands. George Jean Nathan recalled meeting the gay pair just arrived from a foray. Thirty melons were lined up on the Knickerbocker Hotel Bar, and behind each of the treasures was a hilarious tale of deftness and daring.[7]

Ade loved people and things: the smells of a German restaurant, stray dogs, shopgirls, beefy policemen, bawling peddlers, cable-car conductors, balky horses, ferris wheels, the junk shops on Canal Street, stenographers, Pullman porters, bootblacks, Clark Street Chinamen, fires—all the perceptions that delight senses hungry for experience. He was a topnotch newspaperman, and Dennis of the *Record* rewarded his excellence by giving him the columns that became available upon the closing of the Chicago World's Fair. Ade's new and unsigned department was called "Stories of the Streets and of the Town," and it made its first appearance on November 20, 1893. In his custody were two columns on the editorial page that consumed between twelve hundred and two thousand words a day. John T. McCutcheon supplied an illustration. Next to Ade's columns appeared "Sharps and Flats" by Eugene Field.

McCutcheon and Ade delighted in their teamwork. To get paid for wandering around Chicago together was a perpetual vacation. McCutcheon brought his sketch pad and roughed out his illustrations on the scene. The friends worked well together with McCutcheon proportioning his artwork to Ade's space requirements. The illustrations complemented the quality and tone of the copy.

They wandered aimlessly through the streets and around the town like a couple of talented schoolboys on a stolen holiday. Full of high spirits, enthusiasm, and the drive of youth, they sacked Chicago of its sights and sounds, its smells and its characters, its crudeness and its sentimentality. They reveled in orgies of eavesdropping, ogling, and calculated gossip. They drew out shoeblacks, needled the cop on the beat, soft-soaped politicians, pumped street-car conductors, researched the business of bartenders, snooped backstage at the Olympic Theater, joked with charwomen, egged on smart aleck delivery boys, laughed at the stories of Pullman porters, followed the fire engines, rode the cable cars, inspected boardinghouses, visited junk shops, gawked at museums of freaks, and kidded with waitresses, barbers, actors, hotel clerks, and tugboat captains.

They probed Chicago with keen minds and sharp eyes, producing stories about the fish market, the cost of living in a boardinghouse, horse races, city parks, Chinese laundries, restaurants, peddlers, the lake front, evangelists, whisker designers, the coroner's office, and the shops of Chicago.

III *Seven Years*

The readers of the *Record* approved of "Stories of the Streets and of the Town," and Ade found himself a star reporter. He was a prolific writer, a gifted observer, and had a splendid faculty for seeing beauty in simplicity and pattern in commonplace details. With a puff, he could re-create a street-corner character; with a few deft touches, make him everyman's friend; and with a smile of words, fix a moment of his existence. His gay pastiches had a blithe, breezy, affable air that won readers and held them throughout the seven years that "Stories of the Streets and of the Town" lived in the Chicago *Record*.

The department became the talk of Chicago, and the *Record* exploited the popularity of the series by offering a collection in paperback form. Sales were encouraging, and between April, 1894, and July, 1900, eight collections entitled *Stories of the Streets and of the Town* appeared.[8] Neither Ade nor McCutcheon was credited on the title page, although they were widely known as the authors.

Ranging from serious commentary to humorous fiction, Ade's stories are rich in variety. They originally appeared without titles, but this deficiency was corrected in the reprints. A few of Ade's titles are: "The Greeks of Chicago," "Inspector Shea Talks about Criminals," "Queer Ways of Making a Living," "Visitors' Day at the Jail," "City Suicides," "Life on a River Tug," and "Mr. Benson's Experiences with a Maniac."

The piece entitled "Mr. Benson's Experiences with a Maniac," is one of Ade's most enduring tales. Mr. Benson, a medical student who enjoys visiting the county insane asylum, asks to see the violent patients. The assistant warden accompanies Benson through the ward, and, while he is momentarily occu-

pied, Mr. Benson has an adventure. Benson smiles at an inmate of prodigious size and strength. In a twinkling the maniac breaks for Benson, whose reflexes prove excellent. He bolts for South Chicago with the maniac just ten feet behind:

> Benson ran as one whose life was at stake. He was guided only by his terror. As he sped along the hallway he heard the heavy footfalls of the crazy giant, who seemed to be gaining at every step, and who, as he ran, kept up a hoarse gurgling which sometimes rose into a shriek of demoniacal laughter.
>
> "Help! help" gasped Benson, as he threw his whole weight against a door which suddenly appeared before him. He clutched the knob with both hands and wrenched it fiercely.
>
> Thank heaven! It flew open. He dived half-way across the room.

Benson runs on and on, his breath burning his throat, his blood pounding in his head from exertion and terror. He plunges through a window in a frenzy to escape. Torn and bleeding, he scampers desperately across the grounds:

> Benson staggered as he ran and the landscape reeled before his eyes. What was that? Again the demon shrieks—a shriek of triumph; for Benson was running toward a high board fence.
>
> He saw it and cried aloud in awful fear, but he still ran. He leaped for the fence and threw one arm over it. With all his remaining strength he attempted to scramble to the top.
>
> Too late! Too late!
>
> He felt a hand on his back and heard a voice close to his ear: "You're it! You're it! Now see if you can catch me."[9]

From the breathless pace and suspense of "Mr. Benson's Experiences with a Maniac," Ade swings, with equal virtuosity, to "Effie Whittlesy," an exercise in social contrasts. In "Effie Whittlesy" Ade brings the provincialism of the village and the shallowness of the city into sharp focus. In this tale, Ed Wallace learns that his wife has hired a new housekeeper fresh from the country. To his surprise and to his wife's astonishment, the new girl, Effie Whittlesy, is an old friend. Both Ed and Effie were brought up in the same town, but Ed had abandoned the farm for Chicago many years ago. Ed wavers momentarily between his status as an employer and his obligations as a friend. The contest is unequal, and he and Effie shake hands and reminisce, to the consternation of Mrs. Wallace, a sputtering witness to the collapse of civilization. She orders Effie to the kitchen and catechizes her husband on his conduct with a servant. He replies:

"Now, don't ask me to put on any airs with one of the Whittlesys, because they know me from away back. Effie has seen me licked at school. She has been at our house, almost like one of the family, when mother was sick and needed another girl. If my memory serves me right, I've taken her to singing-school and exhibitions. So I'm in no position to lord it over her, and I wouldn't do it anyway. I'd hate to have her go back to Brainerd and report that she met me here in Chicago and I was too stuck up to remember old times and requested her to address me as "Mr. Wallace."

Mrs. Wallace, a Twombley from Baltimore with relatives in Virginia, breathes through her nose and probes her husband's defenses. Ed retreats to the kitchen to talk over old times with Effie. While Mrs. Wallace, née Twombley, shudders at the social atrocity taking place in her kitchen, Ed turns the conversation to the problem facing them both. He offers to pay Effie's way back to Brainerd for a month's vacation and promises to find her a job if she wishes to return to Chicago:

"Well—to tell you the truth, Effie, you see—you're an old friend of mine and I don't like the idea of your being here in my house as a—well, as a hired girl."

"No, I guess I'm a servant now. I used to be a hired girl when I worked for your ma, but now I'm a servant. I don't see as it makes any difference what you call me, as long as the work's the same."

"You understand what I mean, don't you? Any time you come here to my house I want you to come as an old acquaintance— a vis'tor, not a servant."

"Ed. Wallace, don't be foolish. I'd as soon work for you as any one, and a good deal sooner."

"I know, but I wouldn't like to see my wife giving orders to an old friend, as you are. You understand, don't you?"[10]

Effie understands and leaves for Brainerd with an invitation to pay the Wallaces a visit on her return to Chicago. Mrs. Wallace is aghast at the preposterous invitation, but "the revulsion came and . . . with a full return of pride in her husband," she bows to his wishes.

Effie and Ed are depicted with kindly understanding, and even Mrs. Wallace is drawn with a lightness of touch that scores her intolerance and snobbery without making her despicable. The dialogue, nimble and swift, reveals character through both phrase and tone. Few of Ade's later pieces have the emotional intensity or the dimensional characterization of "Effie Whittlesy."

Ade worked diligently to get variety into his department. He wrote social history, burlesque, satire, fables, parodies, dialogues, sketches, tales, short stories, verse, and episodes in the lives of several recurring characters. One of these last, "Clarence Allen, the Hypnotic Boy Journalist," is a burlesque of the dime novels which were still popular in the 1890's. Its spare style and brilliant use of incongruous detail are typical of Ade's ability to step up the voltage of his ludicrous effects. Here, in its entirety, is Chapter V of "Clarence Allen":

> The *Daily Beacon,* like all other great newspapers, had a pack of genuine Siberian bloodhounds, to be used for tracking criminals.
>
> Our hero, after making out an expense account, selected two of the largest and fiercest bloodhounds and showed them the plaster cast of the footprint which he had taken at the Hare residence.
>
> The intelligent animals knew at a glance what was expected of them, and in a few moments they were on the scent, followed by our alert young hero, Clarence Allen, the hypnotic boy journalist, who carried a revolver tightly clenched in his right hand.
>
> For nearly an hour no one spoke.
>
> Then the dogs stopped in front of an old stone house, with tall elms surrounding it.
>
> "This is the place," said Clarence Allen, concealing himself in a thicket to await developments.
>
> After a few moments he chanced to look around, and his blood froze in his veins.
>
> Someone had stolen the dogs![11]

In addition to making his department go, Ade occasionally assisted Amy Leslie, the dramatic editor of the *Record.* He had no ambition to be a critic; his principal interest lay in free tickets. To finance a European trip, both Ade and McCutcheon had asked the paymaster to withhold ten dollars a week from their salary. This enforced savings made free theater tickets powerfully attractive. Ade was temperamentally unfit for dramatic criticism, and he clearly recognized his deficiencies: "I was no good as a dramatic critic," he wrote, "because I was sympathizing with the actors all the time when I should have been shooting arrows into them. I never could get enjoyment from a play so bad that it was supposed to be amusing. All I could see was a group of conscientious, willing and hard-working performers trying to get results from impossible material and meager talents."[12]

The trip to Europe eventuated, and "Stories of the Streets and of the Town" was taken over by Ray Stannard Baker. Charlie Williams replaced McCutcheon as illustrator.

Ade wrote articles from abroad which appeared twice a week in the *Record* under the title "What a Man Sees Who Goes Away from Home." Wherever he traveled—and he visited Ireland, Holland, Belgium, England, Switzerland, Germany, France, and Italy—he reported what he saw and heard with sincere interest and with a desire to be as informative as humorous. He wrote of his ship companions, street sights in London, Italian lotteries, restaurants and pubs, cabbies, prices at the London theaters, the fair at Amsterdam, foreign railways, Waterloo, the Rhine, foreign currency, the gondoliers' union, and "The Polite Art of Smuggling."

IV *Toward Realism*

Upon his return to Chicago, Ade picked up his old department and looked around for new sources of material. He found one idea in Charlie Williams who peppered his speech with slang. Williams' colorful language delighted Ade and led him to create Artie Blanchard whose adventures became popular in the columns. The freshness, brashness, and brass-bound opportunism of young Blanchard were instantly popular; for Artie was everyman's office boy and every other man's son. He epitomized young Chicago with his disarming grin, his fast talk, and his imaginative schemes for instant wealth. Artie wanted everything that life had to offer—and as quickly as possible. His was a speckled soul crouching behind a gold-plated heart. Cunning in the ways of the city, knowing in matters of practical conduct, and captivating in his personality, Artie was also pragmatic, cynical, shallow, and worldly. He had the potential of becoming a classic scoundrel.

These qualities, plus a breezy charm and a refreshing candor, made him precisely the kind of American boy that every Ameri-

can girl wants a crack at reforming. Artie finds such a girl in
Mamie, and he reveals himself to her freely: "I'm workin' for
a square fellow," he says,

> He's *all* right. I used to give him all kinds o' hot and cold
> roasts, but since he went to the front for me and got my salary
> whooped I've got to be with him. I'll tell you, Mame, he's this
> kind. If you'd go up to Morton to-morrow and say: "How about
> it; can you take hold and run the earth for a year?" he'd put on
> one o' them dead easy smiles and say he could do it without
> turnin' a hair. He's got the nerve to tackle anything. He don't
> know nothin', but he don't need to as long he can make suckers
> think he's all right. There's Miller I've told you so much about.
> He knows more about the business than Morton ever wanted to
> know, but Morton draws more stuff just because Miller ain't
> got the face. So I've got wise to this fact; No matter what
> you've got in your hand play it as if you had a royal flush for a
> bosom holdout. I weaken on no proposition. If they wanted me
> to be president o' the whole shootin' match, I'd jump in, grow
> some side-whiskers and put up as tall a con game as that old
> stiff we've got down there now. His office hours is from 11:00 to
> 11:30 and he ain't nothin' but a hamrester when he *is* there.[13]

Artie crackles with slang, flippant patter, and racy wisecracks.
For years the public's appetite for Ade's fireworks was insatiable,
and his reputation and fortune were nailed to his ability to put
old words to new uses and to fabricate new words that shocked
the starch out of hackneyed ideas. His keen ear rejoiced in
exuberant phrases, vivacious words, and grotesque images. He
gathered slang by the tun, strained it of impurities, boosted
its spirit, and ladled it neat into his columns. His readers,
drunk with hilarity, delighted in the ease with which Ade's
language peeled the varnish off traditional values.

His slang was magnificently profane: "The best slang is not
only ingenious and amusing," wrote H. L. Mencken, "it also
embodies a kind of social criticism. It not only provides new
names for a series of everyday concepts, some new and some old;
it also says something about them."[14] Ade's slang reached its
satiric height in the fables, but it learned to fly in *Artie*:

> "Well, I goes," said Artie.
> "Where?" asked Miller, who had forgotten.
> "Where? Well, that's a good thing. To the church show—the
> charity graft. I didn't do a thing but push my face in there
> about eight o'clock last night, and I was 'it' from the start. Say,

I like that church, and if they'll put in a punchin' bag and a plunge they can have my game, I'll tell you those.

"Did you see Mrs. Morton?"

"How's that, boy? Did I see her? Say, she treated me out o' sight. She meets me at the door, puts out the glad hand and says: 'Hang up your lid and come into the game.'"

"I never heard her talk like that," suggested Miller.

"Well, that's what she meant. She's all right, too, and the only wonder to me is how she ever happened to tie herself up to that slob."[15]

Artie was a crude beginning, but Ade's fresh use of American speech earned him the critical attention which spurred his improvement. His next collection, *Pink Marsh,* marks an advance over the glib emptiness of *Artie,* but not until *Doc' Horne* was Ade able to offer a series of meaty sketches that held to the bone.

Pink Marsh (1897) is a colored version of *Artie.* Pink is a sly, likable, garrulous bootblack with all the stereotyped attributes of the nineteenth-century Negro. Truth is merely a starting point from which Pink charts an imaginative course. He is crafty, humorous, full of foxy philosophy, a master crapshooter; he plays the policy numbers, loves wild clothes, big words and strong drink, steals chickens, makes love to the sweet young things, but eventually marries a widow of "p'opehty." Pink is a superstitious, simple-minded, transparent character upon whom the "Morning Customer" sharpens his day.

The Morning Customer primes Pink with tips, and the bootblack rambles from topic to topic. Pink matches Artie's opinions on bicycles, bloomers, and graft with his own dialect commentary on boxing, love, and cake-walks. The Morning Customer usually drops a big word into the conversation to enjoy Pink's rhapsody. In one episode Pink compliments the Morning Customer on his coat:

"Well, I'm glad you like it. It's always a satisfaction to have one's dress approved by a gentleman of taste, and discrimination."

"Hush, man, don't lift me too high. It ain't ev'y culled boy 'at gets 'at lang'age used on him, is it?"

"No sir, that is a special eulogium."

"I jus' see 'at one when it go past me. 'Logeum'—'logeum'— misteh, you got a new one to toss at me ev'y time you come in heah, an' none of 'em ain't so wuhse. 'At's a fact, seh. Some is wahmeh 'an othehs, but ev'y one of 'em smikes."

"That is very kind of you to say so."

"I guess you don' know how to use a cullud pusson good, neetheh. W'y misteh, some days afteh you come in heah an' give me 'at kind o' convehsation, I feel 'at if I had mo' ej'cation I wouldn' be rubbin' no man's shoes no, seh. I'd be lawyeh o' someping like 'at."[16]

The episodic structure of both *Artie* and *Pink Marsh* results in a series of incidents, anecdotes, and conversations; for Ade made no attempt to integrate the sketches or to build anything more than a matchstick house of racy dialogues and picturesque observations. True, he depicted the city Negro and the urban drugstore cowboy, but his portraits were superficial. In his columns Ade skimmed the surface of the city, laughed genially at its absurdities, its poses, its self-important pursuits, and its shallowness. Although his stories had fascination, they were spun from glibness and literary sleight-of-hand. Ade was a one-armed piano player who, though marvelously dexterous, was limited in his repertoire.

Time and time again the Morning Customer minces into the downstairs barbershop and mounts the bootblack's throne. Waiting across the room behind a newspaper is George Ade with ears poised. The insufferable Morning Customer begins to play upon Pink as though he were a steam calliope. Every note is true, every response elicited perfectly, the tip is flipped, and the Morning Customer swaggers off glowing with superiority. Read in spaced episodes in the *Record,* the stories about Pink were fun; but *Pink Marsh* at a sitting is painful in the extreme.

Doc' Horne (1899) hangs together better than *Pink Marsh,* for Ade, who began to take his collections more seriously, rewrote and polished the newspaper pieces for book publication. In addition, he wrote the last five chapters especially for the book. Greater unity of tone was the result in *Doc' Horne,* and, though its episodic structure is unchanged, Ade improved his transitions between episodes. In consequence the character of Doc' Horne takes on a reality that, while hardly three dimensional, is at least quality pasteboard. Doc'—a lovable old duffer, harmless, windy, entertaining—has an expansiveness that propounds all abilities and wisdom. He may be just a roomer at the Alfalfa European Hotel in the cheap-rent district of Chicago, but his past has been glorious, his experiences widespread and rich. Doc's generosity is prodigal in advice, knowledge, and the recital of his achievements.

The book teems with tall tales, fine miniature portraits, ingenious observation, and crisp dialogue. Undoubtedly Ade's most
memorable character, Doc' Horne lingers in the mind longer
than any other Ade creature; for this loquacious, testy, colorful
old fraud has a Dickensian flair that rescues him from oblivion.
Unlike Pink Marsh, who was a buck-and-wing caricature, there
is blood in the old man. He is as kind as he is windy; as sensitive as he is vain. His fellow roomers shower upon him their
respect and occasionally their suspicion, and Doc' blooms or
bristles accordingly. His auditors and friends are a motley group
of shabby-genteel roomers: the "lush," the lightning dentist,
the actor, the race-track man, the hustler, the drummer, the
book-agent, and the freckled boy who is a geyser of slang.

With detail-laden phrases, Ade tagged his characters with
attributes that have the subtle twist of satire. Doc', for instance,
was temporarily impressed by the book-agent, a Johnsonian
personage:

> . . . he was large, and he had whiskers, and it is known that
> many a politician has gone to congress and many a doctor has
> built up a country practice with no other qualifications than
> these two. The book-agent wore a somewhat faded Prince Al-
> bert coat, which supported his assumption of learning and pro-
> fessional dignity.
>
> The stringy side whiskers were lightly streaked with gray, and
> the growing baldness was only half-concealed by a long wisp
> of hair which was brought up from the side and spread across
> the bare patch. The book-agent spoke rather slowly, biting off
> his words with the precision of a hardened school teacher. During
> the first hour with him one would be led to believe that he
> had spent his life among the poets. His conversation was liter-
> ally stuffed with gems of verse. After a second or third meeting
> with him it became apparent that he repeated himself, calling
> up the same quotation twice or thrice in the same week. The
> lush, who was an observant person during his lucid intervals,
> concluded, after three weeks, that the book-agent had a limited
> repertoire of verses and couplets which he had learned from book
> prospectuses. This conclusion was borne out by a study of the
> agent's outfit which he carried with him. He had a prospectus
> of the "Sweet Singers of All Time," giving sample pages and
> illustrations, and the lush found, on looking through it one day,
> that all the stray bits of poetry which the learned book-agent
> casually called to mind were in this concealed volume. . . .

Besides, he was so conscious of his own learning. He smiled
indulgently on the bicycle salesman, even as he quoted Shake-

speare, and all his intercourse was marked by a calm and
thoughtful politeness. He had the habit of patting and rubbing
himself in front as if to quiet the seething emotions of his soul.[17]

Doc' is a kindly busybody bent on doing good and collecting
esteem. He tries to reform the lush, to find a suitable mate for
the lightning dentist, and to advise the hustler who eventually
victimizes him. Equal to most occasions, however, Doc's opinions
carry great weight with the roomers.

The old man has his setbacks, for he prickles with dignity.
But, when his sovereignty is unchallenged, he beams with Pick-
wickian benignity as he explains how to protect oneself against
footpads, to live among the Southern aristocracy, to handle large
sums of money, to beat a bully, to advise the Secretary of War,
and to excel at marksmanship. The roomers hold Doc' in genuine
affection, for there is a dram of magic in the old fraud. They
would protect him from exposure if possible; and, when he
comes perilously close to being found out, the suspense is painful.

The gallery of characters in *Doc' Horne*, realistically portrayed,
quickly won the respect of Howells and other realists who were
eager for the development of this fresh young talent. But Ade
had a problem to solve, and his solution turned him from the
path of realism.

Ade was a resourceful, inventive journalist, yet he was chal-
lenged by the curse of the columnist: variety for his readers.
"Stories of the Streets and of the Town" is an admirable example
of how Ade succeeded in solving his problem. One of Ade's most
important ventures in the pursuit of novelty was a literary ex-
periment, a fable in slang, that appeared in his department on
September 17, 1897. It became the cornerstone of his fame, the
windfall of his wealth, and the millstone of his talent.

CHAPTER 3

The Fabulous Fabulist

"The fellow is a genius, at least in the *Fables*.
His language is a creation, like Shakespeare's.
He does not use slang, he makes it, and can
there be a more splendid creative effort of the
human spirit?"

—Gamaliel Bradford

"I would rather have written
Fables in Slang than be President."

—William Allen White

ADE GAVE the ancient form of the fable a sharp twist by
retaining the archaic form and stilted manner and by steeping it in colloquial language generously laced with slang. The result was linguistic fire.

His first fable appeared in the Chicago *Record* with the half apologetic title "This is a Fable." Later it was included in *Fables in Slang* (1900), but with extensive revisions as "The Fable of Sister Mae, Who Did as Well as. Could Be Expected."

The first fable in slang went well, but Ade didn't write another for a month, and the second fable was free of slang. About this time Ade's publisher asked him to produce an original book-length work, and Ade proposed a novel to be called *The College Widow*. He outlined the plot, primed his conscience with excellent intentions, stocked up on soft lead pencils and reams of the yellow paper on which he wrote, and then bogged down. He couldn't feed his hungry columns and write a novel on the side. He had written two more fables that were widely quoted, and the publisher, despairing of the novel, suggested that a collection of fables might do just as well. Eager to be released of his obligation, Ade geared himself to fabricate fables. He had the profitable faculty of gauging public taste, and each of his fables whetted an appetite for more. By the time he had enough to make a book, his readers had become addicts. Moreover, Ade found that fables in slang were a joy to write. No longer hampered by the conventions, he entered upon a debauch of literary free love, which, though immensely satisfying, ultimately exacted a price.

One of Ade's briefest fables, and an excellent one to use as an example, is "The Fable of the Caddy Who Hurt His Head Thinking":

> One day a Caddy sat in the Long Grass near the Ninth Hole and wondered if he had a Soul. His Number was 27, and he had almost forgotten his Real name.
>
> As he sat and Meditated, two Players passed him. They were going the Long Round, and the Frenzy was upon them.
>
> They followed the Gutta Percha Balls with the intent swiftness of trained Bird Dogs, and each talked feverishly of Brassy Lies, and getting past the Bunker and Lofting to the Green, and Slicing into the Bramble—each telling his own Game to the Ambient Air, and ignoring what the other Fellow had to say.
>
> As they did the St. Andrews Full Swing for eighty Yards apiece and then Followed Through with the usual explanations of how it Happened, the Caddy looked at them and Reflected that they were much inferior to his Father.
>
> His Father was too serious a Man to get out in Mardi Gras Clothes and hammer a Ball from one Red Flag to another.
>
> His Father worked in a Lumber Yard.
>
> He was an Earnest Citizen, who seldom smiled, and he knew all about the Silver Question and how J. Pierpont Morgan done up a Free People on the Bond Issue.
>
> The Caddy wondered why it was that his Father, a really Great Man, had to shove Lumber all day and could seldom get one Dollar to rub against another, while these superficial Johnnies who played Golf all the Time had Money to Throw at the Birds. The more he Thought the more his Head ached
>
> Moral: *Don't try to Account for Anything.*[1]

Ade had the ability to sound, as on a piccolo, the precise note which piped in a character's soul:

> Once upon a Time there was a slim Girl with a Forehead which was Shiny and Protuberant, like a Bartlett Pear. When asked to put Something in an Autograph Album she invariably wrote the Following, in a tall, dislocated Back-Hand:
>
> "Life is Real; Life is Earnest,
> And the Grave is not its Goal."
> That's the kind of a Girl she was.[2]

This maiden lusted for culture and was tagged by the boys at the drugstore as a "Cold Proposition." Disdaining the local serfs, she waited patiently for her shining knight: "a big and pensive Literary Man, wearing a Prince Albert coat, a neat Derby Hat and godlike Whiskers. When He came he would enfold Her in his Arms and whisper Emerson's Essays to her." Unfortunately he didn't show. Finally at the age of thirty-four she cashed in her intellectual chips and married a janitor by the name of Earnest.

Like silver axes Ade's phrases flew in short graceful arcs to sink with satisfying "chunks" into the heartwood of an idea. There was no weakness or pose or arrogance or idiocy that he could not cut down with an easy chuckle or an incisive grin. His blade was double-edged, too. Take the case of the wealthy do-gooder: "Kindly explain to him," she says to the mother of an underprivileged child,

> that I take an Interest in him, even though he is the Offspring of an Obscure and Ignorant Workingman, while I am probably the Grandest Thing that ever Swept up the Boulevard. I must go now, but I will Return. Next time I come I hope to hear that your husband has stopped Drinking and is very Happy. Tell the Small Person under the Bed that if he learns to spell "Ibex" by the time I call again I will let him look at my Rings. As for you, bear in mind that it is no Disgrace to be Poor; it is simply Inconvenient, that's all.
>
> Having delivered herself of these Helpful remarks she would Duck, and the Uplifted Mother would put a Nickel in the Can and send Lizzie over to the Dutchman's.[3]

Ade's characters were all of common clay. At best they were cynical, at worst they were ridiculous; but they were always human; they were usually funny. He chose typical Americans: the girl who was going to break into society if she had to use an axe, the college boy who made sport of his hayseed friends, the homely girl who did finger exercises on the piano while the beaux stormed the house across the street, the henpecked husband, people with chop house manners, girls who used toothpicks, youths who played mandolins, farm boys who went to Cuba in 1898 and began to shoot at everything that looked foreign, women who loved "Vogner," farmers who stepped on their own feet when in the city, the town boy with a hat lined with satin like a child's coffin, and hundreds of other magnificent nobodies who, in reality, were everybody except the four hundred.

The fables revealed no great spirits nor noble characters, few who were sensible, and fewer who were wise. The characters may be divided roughly, into three classes: the gullible, the trapped, and the cynical; and usually the cynic is the hero, if an Ade fable can be said to have a hero. Much of Ade's popularity was based on this amiable cynicism.

Ade's popularity grew like Jack's beanstalk and virtually overnight he became America's bard of mirth. His fables were sonnets of hilarity lined with sparkling crystals of laughter. There was nothing abstruse about them; their morals were clear. They were written about the common reader and for him, and millions throughout the nation roared with delight at their own follies, futilities, and frustrations. Frequently the fables stepped up from wit to the pedestal of humor with a smile of understanding and a chuckle of enlightenment. For though the fables danced lightly on the surface of life, Ade's schottische revealed deeper layers of existence, too: the loneliness of the farm, the destruction of the village, the emptiness of the city, the inadequacy of traditional values, the tedium of life without laughter, the lust for status and culture, the national distrust of ideas and acceptance of prosperity as an ultimate value.

The fables won their way easily, for their form was familiar and their manner was both novel and irreverent. Ade was a new McGuffey who peppered his reader with slang and reversed all the old values. In the fables, industry and perseverance paid off in calluses; and, if one went to bed early and rose with the dawn, he missed all the prominent people.

The magic of Ade's fables is not found in a formula, in a technique, or in a set of characteristics. They are delectable vignettes lightly marinated in a piquant sauce of satire, parody, absurd logic, puns, anti-climax, alliteration, slang, incongruity, dialect, exaggeration, wisecracks, irony, cynicism, wit, candor, philistinism, spirited epithets, memorable phrases, familiar character types, chuckling disillusionment, common prejudices, and a terse, transparent style reminiscent of a child's primer.

Ade sprinkled all this with a generous helping of capital letters that served a variety of purposes. There is no pattern to Ade's use of capitals. Occasionally he capitalized a cliché to reveal its banality or pomposity, but overall he used capitalization as a typographical device that slowed down the reader, made him savor common words, and forced him to intone the fable in a school-boy rhythm.

A typical opening paragraph is:

> Lutie was an Only Child. When Lutie was eighteen her Mother said they ought to do something with Lutie's Voice. The Neighbors thought so, too. Some recommended killing the Nerve. Others allowed that it ought to be Pulled.[4]

One of Ade's favorite targets was the American posture on culture, education, and ideas. In the following fable, "The Kind of Music That is Too Good for Household Use," Ade's capitalization may be studied and his philistinism illustrated:

> One Evening a little Flock of Our Best People got together at the Home of a Lady who invariably was first over the Fence in the Mad Pursuit of Culture. She loved to fill her Front Rooms with Folks who wore 7¾ Hats and read Norwegian Novels that no one else ever heard anything about.
>
> On the Evening already mentioned she had a Cluster of Geniuses on hand. They were expected to Talk for a couple of Hours, so as to work up an Appetite for Neapolitan Ice-Cream and Lady-Fingers. In the course of time they got around to the Topic of Modern Music. All agreed that the Music which seemed to catch on with the low-browed Public was exceedingly punk. They rather fancied "Parcifal" and were willing to concede that Vogner made good in Spots, but Mascagni they branded as a Crab. As for Victor Herbert and J. P. Sousa—back to the Water-Tanks!
>
> A little later in the Game the Conversation began to sag and it was suggested that they have Something on the Piano. They gathered around the Stack of Music and then Vogner went into the Discard and Puccini fell to the floor unnoticed and the Classics did not get a Hand. But they gave a Yelp of Joy when they spotted a dear little Cantata about a Coon who carried a Razor and had trouble with his Wife. They sang the Chorus 38 times and the Young Lady wore out both Wrists doing Rag-Time.
>
> MORAL: It is proper to enjoy the Cheaper Grades of Art, but they should not be formally Indorsed.[5]

Championing the national suspicion of ideas and eggheads, Ade wrote a number of fables about the "culture game," "the brain hatcheries" and their professors, and the absurdities of the educational experiments then popular. In "The Fable of

The Old-Time Pedagogue Who Came Down from the Shelf and Was Sufficiently Bumped," Ade took a healthy swing at progressive education. In this fable a country school teacher, long retired, substitutes for his daughter who is ill. He asks the class which of the three R's they would like to tackle first, and he is given the horse-laugh. In exasperation he asks the class about their course of study:

> "I will give you a few Points, seeing that you are stalled," said a very small Urchin. "First we design Wall-Paper, then we dissect a Rat, after which we have French and Calisthenics, and finish up with a few Stunts in Botany and Entomology."
>
> "What in the Name of all Git-Out is Entomology?" interrogated the Old-timer.
>
> At this Bad Break there was more Scornful Laughter. The Little People certainly had the Old-timer looking like Mexican Money with Holes in it. Every time they knocked him a twister he Fumbled it and fell over in the Tall Grass.
>
> "Back to the Mines, Grandpa!" shouted one Roguish Youngster in the Back Row.
>
> Then all of them began to Talk about him in French, which he could not understand. They said he was a Hommard, the same being French for Lobster.
>
> "Stop all this Hifalutin' Tomfoolery," exclaimed the Old-timer, with Rising Anger. "Talk United States and don't Jabber. How are you on the Spell?"
>
> "We don't Monkey with Spelling any more," replied the Boy. "We simply start in and learn to Read the first Crack out of the Box."[6]

Ade had come to enjoy the reputation of being a warm-hearted satirist: one with no snarl or bite. On the whole this description is true, but there are a few passages in his fables that are not warm-hearted. Jonathan Swift would have envied "The Fable of the Honest Money-Maker and the Partner of His Joys, Such as They Were," and Hamlin Garland, though no satirist, would have given the piece a standing ovation. The Honest Money-Maker is Henry, a prosperous farmer with herds of fat animals, a healthy bank account, and a big barn. His farm machinery was in perfect condition, and the respect of his neighbors was high. Also, Henry had a wife and children. Henry's wife, carefully selected for health and durability, was then "put into his Kitchen to serve the Remainder of her Natural Life." Ade details her life on the farm:

After ten years of raising Children, Steaming over the Wash-tub, Milking the Cows, Carrying in Wood, Cooking for the Hands, and other Delsarte such as the Respected Farmer usually Frames Up for his Wife, she was thin as a Rail and humped over in the Shoulders. She was Thirty, and looked Sixty. Her Complexion was like Parchment and her Voice had been worn to a Cackle. She was losing her Teeth, too, but Henry could not afford to pay Dentist Bills because he needed all his Money to buy more Poland Chinas and build other Cribs. If she wanted a Summer Kitchen or a new Wringer or a Sewing Machine, or Anything Else that would lighten her Labors, Henry would Moan and Grumble and say she was trying to land him in the Poorhouse.

. . . .

The wife of the Respected Farmer was the only Work Animal around the Place that was not kept Fat and Sleek. But, of course, Henry did not count on Selling her.[7]

Now Henry was pious, patriotic, and prosperous. He was businesslike and didn't dally in foreclosing mortgages or using child labor; so he was eminently successful. One afternoon "he was out Dickering for a Bull, and his Woman, lying on the cheap Bedstead, up under the hot Roof, folded her lean Hands and slipped away to the only Rest she had known since she tied up with a Prosperous and Respected Farmer." Inside of a month Henry was out looking for another. (His daughter was only eleven and not big enough to do the chores.) He found a healthy one, and the papers referred to them as "the happy couple."

Here is the bite and bile of a satiric indignation that etches upon the conscience with the fire of acid. America chuckled over the gentle satire of George Ade; but it might have been scourged magnificently had the insuperable geniality been crushed from Ade's soul.

Ade's fables are dated principally by their slang and the virtual disappearance of the chasm that once separated the city from the country. Ade pounded the village with a slapstick: "Out in the Celery Belt of the Hinterland there is a stunted Flag-Station. . . . In this Settlement the Leading Citizens still wore gum Arctics with large Buckles, and Parched Corn is served at Social Functions."[8] The farm towns are named Fodder-ville, Miasma, Smartweed Junction, Sleepy Hollow, Nubbinville, and Dinkusville. Ade was keenly interested in their escapees and what happened to them when they broke into the city.

Through his caricatures of rubes and slickers, he contrasted the dreariness of the farm with the excitement of the city. Dickensian in vitality and variety, his city-country types lack, however, the opulence and memorable individuality of Dickens' people; and the Moral of their brief lives is also their epitaph.

Much of the criticism that dismisses Ade with an impatient gesture points out that most of his language has slipped into the limbo of lost words. True, many of his slang terms are now obscure (gazimbat, throw a double Arab, swing into the mazy, and Tiffany water), but most of his slang is still current or understandable (slow-poke, dippy, fly the coop, foxy, the long green, keen, and piffle). Despite his eagerness to exploit the vernacular of the streets, Ade developed a set of standards to govern his use of slang:

> I never referred to a policeman as a bull, because that word belongs to the criminal vocabulary, and Mother and the girls are not supposed to be familiar with the cryptic terms of yeggmen. I never referred to a young girl as a *chicken*. The word originated in the deepest pits of white slavery, and it always gave me the creeps. A young girl may be a *flapper*, a *bud*, a *peach*, a *pippin*, a *lollypaloozer*, a *nectarine*, a *cutie*, a *queen*, *the one best bet*, a *daisy*, or even a *baby doll*, without being insulted, but never a *chicken*, unless one is writing a treatise on social problems.[9]

Ade's slang dates the fables but it does not out-date them. There is not enough unintelligible slang to choke their verve and freshness. Colloquialisms and unconventional expression by far outweigh slang in Ade's ten volumes of fables. Too, he shocks with outlandish images which have the tone if not the form of slang: "He got what seems to be due every Brakeman. He was a little slow in withdrawing the Left Fin and the Bumpers caught him. When he came out of the Hospital his Left Hand looked like a Pair of Scissors."[10] And there was the member of the Silver Cornet Band who "carried a Tuby that looked like the Entrance to a Cave."[11]

Ade's sentences are lean and supple; his images are impudent exaggerations of the commonplace; his precision in word-choice, excellent; his timing, superb; his caricatures, sharp and vital; his communication, clear; and his message, unmistakable. Few humorists surpassed Ade in literary talent, but though he had impressive gifts, he sold his abundance by the pound and grew rich rather than great.

William Dean Howells pleaded with Ade to turn his back on journalism and to develop his genius, "but," wrote Ade, "he who becomes corrupted by the unearned increment is simply hungry for more swag."[12] In a weak moment he toyed with turning to purposeful realism:

I have promised William Dean Howells, in a never-to-be-forgotten interview, that I will further consecrate my efforts to unadorned realism. But, hang it all, the circus vernacular brings in more royalties than "Artie," "Pink Marsh" and "Doc' Horne" all put together. The dollar sign is luminous in the sky. Another good man gone wrong.[13]

For more than forty years Ade wrote fables (the last appeared in 1939),[14] but his abundant energies prodded him into other literary enterprises. His pen was tipped in gold; and, in the first decade of the twentieth century, he invested his talents in Broadway—the Wall Street of literary fortunes. The dividends were handsome.

CHAPTER *4*

Whistling Down Broadway

> I recall the happy days when I received a
> sheaf of royalty checks every week and my
> father, at the bank down in Indiana, thought
> I had turned out to be a burglar. It just
> seemed as if everyone in the world was slap-
> ping me in the face with twenty dollar bills.
>
> —"The Hardest $100,000 That I
> Ever Earned."

GEORGE ADE exploded over Broadway like a star shell,
burning for a moment with breath-taking brilliance before
a dimming descent to extinction. Within three years Ade became
one of the most luminous lights of the American theater. Fame
and immense fortune were his votaries, and the celebrities of
New York's gay way eagerly admitted him to their circle. But
the light dimmed: before a decade had passed, Ade was a has-
been with the finest set of playbills and theatrical memorabilia
to be found in the cornbelt.

Two years after *The Sultan of Sulu* was produced in 1902,
Ade was the honored guest at a testimonial dinner at Delmonico's
sponsored by the American Dramatist's Club. A hundred of his
peers gathered to do him honor. Playgoers paid tribute at the
box office to the hottest property in the American theater: in
December 1904, for instance, Ade had three plays on Broadway
and two on the road. His productiveness and success prompted
the humorist Charles Battell Loomis to write:

> I am sorry to say that with the coming of the New Year I made
> a resolve that will be hurtful to you. I decided to write a play
> before the year should close, but with the start you have already
> it will take me some time to distance you.
> And, anyhow, isn't this country big enough for you and me?
> *I* believe there is money in unwholesome plays. I believe that

if I can write bucolic plays full of eroticism and lust and evil concupiscence and desire that the back bone of the Republic will flock to them. Just because you have hit it with clean plays is no reason for thinking that I can't hit it with unclean ones. Look at Pinero. I know stories just as good as that of the dancing doll (called the bobbing apple when I heard it) and I'll build up plays around them so that every drummer who goes to see them will be able to laugh at his special favorite and assure his wife that I don't mean what he means and then refuse to tell her what the meaning is. Why I can pack all the disreputable theaters in the country.

If one tenth of the people who have been amused at a filthy joke come to see my plays I will make more money in one week than you do in six days.

Willy Winter may denounce me but the rest of the New York critics will laud me to the skies.

Go on if you will with your clean and wholesome and true nature plays. I'll be unclean and unhealthy and true to nature.

Your plays would not have caught the public so hard twelve years ago. The swing of the pendulum from the French stuff lifted you up and landed you in public favor. I'll make the pendulum swing harder and you can keep landing just as long as you continue to write plays that I can take my daughter to. But I'll write the kind that my son wouldn't dare take me to and I'll advertise them as appealing to the prurient.[1]

In addition to approving the wholesomeness of his plays, the critics hailed Ade for performing a great service for the theater "by demonstrating the stupidity, vulgarity, and uselessness of the horse play and dialectic idiocy which are pulling the lighter forms of legitimate drama down to the level of the variety stage."[2]

I *Theater Crazy*

Ade's interest in theater was voracious and undiscriminating. From boyhood he had been delighted with spectacles that splashed color upon the dullness of the backwoods. The big top was a passion, the Swiss bell-ringers a delight; he thrilled to the magic-lantern lecturers and the itinerant players "who did things to 'East Lynne' and 'Lady Audley's Secret,' and on Saturday evening presented a silver fruit dish to the holder of the lucky ticket."[3]

Ade's imagination had been hungry for any sight or sound or experience which stirred the Kentland corn. "All my life I have been theater-crazy," he wrote. "The top prices at our local temple of Thespis ran to $1.50 per parquet seat for very good attractions. Front seats in the gallery brought fifty cents and the elevated section, crowding the roof and commonly designated as 'nigger heaven,' brought twenty-five cents a seat, and you had to find your own seat, because the patrons were crowded on long, hard wooden benches. Crouched within that suffocating region, just under the rafters, I became acquainted with the greatest dramatic artists of the closing quarter of the nineteenth century."[4]

At Kentland and later at the Grand Opera House in Lafayette, Ade saw many of the popular actors of the day. Most of the productions were by the "rep" companies working out of Indianapolis: the Riley Company, Graham Earle Stock, and the Harry Hotto Players, which to the Midwest were Frohman, Daly, and Belasco.

The Harrigan and Hart song books were popular with Ade, and he collected the "mushy ballads" of the Grant and Hayes administrations. He developed a passion for Gilbert and Sullivan, and, as late as 1925, he claimed not to have missed a performance of *The Mikado* in forty years.

Although he gained his foothold on Broadway through musical comedy, Ade disdained the form and disparaged his work in the genre. "A good musical comedy consists largely of disorderly conduct occasionally interrupted by talk," he wrote. "The man who provides the interruptions is called the librettist. I would advise any man who hasn't the nerve to be a foot-pad or is too large to get through a transome, to become a librettist." The music "must be the kind that any messenger boy can learn to whistle after hearing it twice." As for the dialogue: "It must be guaranteed to wring boisterous laughter from the three-dollar patron who has a facial angle of thirty degrees, and a cerebellum about the size of an olive; also it must have sufficient literary quality and subtle humour to please the dead-head who is sitting in the fourth row with a hammer in one hand and a javelin in the other."[5]

In spite of his opinions about musical comedy in general, Ade modeled his first successful work, *The Sultan of Sulu,* on the Gilbert and Sullivan pattern and took Broadway by storm. Following the *Sultan,* he wrote *Peggy from Paris,* another musical. These plays were primarily important in leading him to straight comedy where he found purpose, satisfaction, and great financial reward. For Ade made a conscious effort to raise the tone of American comedy: he refused to descend to physical buffoonery, and he refused to use sex for laughter. "If I have any single ambition in reference to the stage," he wrote, "it is to depict every-day American life in such a manner as to amuse the public and not offend good taste."[6]

Greatly favoring plays dealing with American life, Ade had little interest in English society dramas, translations from the German, or adaptations of French farces—except for their usefulness as models for the American playwright. Foreign plays were disproportionately popular in America at the time, and Ade felt this unjust to American dramatists and to theatergoers. He saw America "simply reeking with material all ready to be transplanted to the stage,"[7] and he pointed to James A. Herne, William Gillette, Charles H. Hoyt, Bronson Howard, Augustus Thomas, and Denman Thompson as already having accomplished much in their depiction of American home life.

American types and American wholesomeness were the core of Ade's comedies. Throughout his life he championed clean dramas and homely American types. On May 11, 1926, he wrote:

> For many years I was around the theater and no one could be more interested in the native drama, but conditions have been so churned about that I almost hesitate to express any kind of opinion regarding the stage. Just now a very bold type of play, dealing in a shameless manner with the sex relationship, seems to be popular in a few of the large cities. In spite of this fact, I think we may find satisfaction in recalling that the important successes in the theater and the long runs and the huge profits have been marked up for plays which are absolutely clean and wholesome and which, strangely enough, depend upon "atmosphere" and characterization rather than the well-known ingredients such as love interest and intense melodrama. If you talk to a producing manager in regard to a play he will tell you that you must have many throbbing "situations" and a romantic love story as a motif for the construction. But, if you will check up the big successes you will find that a surprising number of them did not deal with youth or romance or love and did not strive for thrilling dramatic climaxes. How about "The Old Homestead," "Rip Van Winkle," and "Lightnin'"? Once I wrote a play called "The County Chairman" which had a mere thread of a love story and consisted mostly of the doings in a small town during a campaign year along about 1880. The play ran

for years. I would not advise a young writer to ignore the so-called love story and I would not argue against the fact that action and conflict are usually the two essentials of a good play. I would tell him, however, that the American public has ever shown a preference for genuine home characters who are placed before a background of naturalness.[8]

Ade's personal experiences bore him out, for two of his own plays were among the most popular of his generation, and his one-act plays still appeal to amateur groups to whom his name is now unfamiliar.

II *False Start*

On January 21, 1901, Ade made his Broadway debut. It was a dismal failure: his play, *The Night of the Fourth,* closed after fourteen performances. Today, little is known about this play. The manuscript is lost, and its disappearance was to Ade one of the mercies of his dramatic career. He wrote:

> I found myself concocting something meant to be a farce comedy, to be called The Night of the Fourth. John Dunne and Tom Ryley were managing Matthews and Bulger, a most popular team of patter comedians and parody singers. The opus was really written for these two stars. It had enough dialogue and connective tissue to hold it together and make it a framework on which to hang songs and dances. Dunne and Ryley took the script out west with them and produced the play in San Francisco before I knew they had accepted it. A telegram brought word that the piece had scored a resounding hit. Then came the newspaper clippings—most complimentary.
> The company worked eastward and I went to St. Paul to look at a performance and bolster up some of the weak spots. . . . It seemed a most sickly and unreal mixture of nothing much. . . . But the house was crowded and many of the lines seemed to score and the producers told me it was really a "vehicle."
> Well, it was a success on the road and a fizzle when done at Hammerstein's Victoria in New York with new scenery, beautiful costumes and a large company. My name was not printed on the bill and I escaped the lambasting which was accorded the play, but I suffered intensely. One critic said The Night of the Fourth made him feel like the morning of the Fifth.[9]

The nature of the play is reflected in the New York reviews. Much, too, is revealed in the names of the characters: Cloyster and Oyster, Miss Cellaneous, Dr. X. Rays Cuticle, etc. Eli Frost, a retired iceman, goes to the country to rest. To insure the tranquility of his retreat, Eli buys up all the fireworks in the village right before the Fourth of July and hides them in the basement of the Summer Rest Hotel. On the day of the big celebration, he goes to the basement to escape whatever noise might yet be devised by determined patriots. Ironically, a single firecracker had eluded his search, and that lone symbol of American independence is lighted and thrown down upon him. The resultant explosion and pyrotechnic display accomplishes the discomfiture and rout of Eli and the other guests of the Summer Rest Hotel.

Keenan Swift, a young lawyer who must raise ten thousand dollars before he can wed the girl of his choice, institutes damage suits on behalf of everyone in the hotel against everyone else and then represents both sides in the dispute. By trick and device, Swift finally extorts the needed money from the retired iceman. One absurd complication tumbles upon another until the climax of the play finds Eli in an insane asylum. According to the reviews, the turbulent and zany conflict is ingeniously resolved with happy consequences to all.

On the whole the reviews of *The Night of the Fourth* ranged from cold disdain to tepid indifference. The New York *Dramatic Mirror* served up the most devastating condemnation: "Absolute drivel, pointless chatter, and purposeless dialogue. Why anyone should have produced such stuff is a question beyond answering."[10]

On the whole the play was dealt with hastily but less harshly in other reviews. The New York *Times* summed up *The Night of the Fourth* in a judgment that seems kind by the slim evidences afforded: "Folks who are fond of this sort of entertainment will like this piece very much and will tell their friends so. Those who do not like high kicking, 'coon' songs and dances, pantomime jokes, and strident music hall voices would best stay away."

Ade sold his rights in the play to Dunne and Ryley for five hundred dollars, and few ever learned that he wrote the farce, an ignorance pleasing to Ade. Actually, however, *The Night of the Fourth* introduced Ade to backstage theater; and, though it soured his taste for playmaking, it taught him techniques which he turned to profit within two years.

III   *Benevolent Assimilation*

The Sultan of Sulu, one of the outstanding box office attractions of the 1902-03 season in New York, was Ade's first stage success. His achievement was remarkable, for only two of the 204 plays produced in New York in the 1902-03 season outran *The Sultan's* 192 performances; and it all happened to Ade in spite of himself.

Ade stumbled on the idea for *The Sultan of Sulu* on one of his trips. In 1900 he spent time in Manila with a group of newspaper correspondents assigned to the Aguinaldo insurrection. They had been to the main island of the Sulu Archipelago, and their yarns about the sultan, his pretentious court, extensive harem, and his disagreement with certain provisos of the American constitution, bubbled in Ade's imagination. John T. McCutcheon, cartoonist and correspondent for the Chicago *Record,* was a member of the group and kept Ade abreast of the American negotiations with Hadji Mohammed Jamalol Ki-Ram, Brother of the Sun and Sultan of Jolo, the principal island of the Sulu Archipelago.[11]

Ade was aware of the comic opera aspects of the material, but he had little inclination, after *The Night of the Fourth,* to write another play. He tried to give the idea to Frank Pixley, the librettist who had written *The Burgomaster.* When Pixley wasn't interested, Ade offered the story of Kirke La Shelle. Turned down again, Ade unsuccessfully tried to interest Lew Dockstader, the minstrelman, in the idea.

Fortunately a young man named Alfred G. Wathall, who had approached Ade for a libretto before his Philippine trip, salvaged the tale from oblivion. Ade's sole activity was to write his weekly syndicated fable, the work of a few hours, and time began to charge his energies. In a kind of desperate boredom he recalled Wathall's request, evoked the shades of Gilbert and Sullivan, and with amazing immediacy *The Sultan of Sulu* took shape.

The play opened in Chicago at the Studebaker Theater on March 9, 1902, and held the boards through May 18, 1902. The tryout soon uncovered the weaknesses in the musical comedy, and the doctoring began. Ade and company revised *The Sultan of Sulu* three or four times, tried out forty-six musical numbers, and finally retained twenty-two. Wilbur D. Nesbit, Ohio-born author and newspaperman, was chosen to polish the lyrics; and *The Sultan of Sulu* again took to the boards, this time on the road with Frank Moulan playing Ki-Ram. The play met with great success, although the doctoring continued. About three weeks after *The Sultan* stormed Broadway, Frank Moulan wrote George Ade: "I contended that if Hannibal and Omaha would take our goods, without the slapstick and the usual trimmings which go with the entertainment they have handed them usually, that New York must take it, or lose its self respect. I have been vindicated, thank Ade. . . . Suffice to say we have landed on 'em so hard that Bdway hasn't recovered yet from the blow and I know that you cannot possibly realize the extent of your personal hit as librettist."[12]

In spite of his intentions to the contrary, Ade was forced to spice *The Sultan of Sulu* with slang, frivolous song and dance routines, and sumptuous production numbers. Ade wrote: "We have compromised by inserting a few 'popular numbers,' on the plea that 'the people in front want it.' "[13]

The Sultan of Sulu is a spoof of America's imperialistic policies in the Philippine Islands. Sulu and its Sultan, Ki-Ram, are to be assimilated quietly but thoroughly. American troops land upon the island under the command of Colonel Jefferson Budd of the Volunteers, and the capitulation of Ki-Ram is immediately effected:

BUDD. We are your friends. We have come to take possession of the island and teach your benighted people the advantages of free government. We hold that all government derives its just powers from the consent of the governed.

ALL. Hear! Hear!

BUDD. Now, the question is, do you consent to this benevolent plan?

(The soldiers bring their guns to "charge bayonets." Ki-Ram looks right and left and finds himself walled in by threatening weapons. He hesitates.)

KI-RAM. Are all the guns loaded?

BUDD. They *are*.

KI-RAM. I consent.[14]

Having secured the subjection of Sulu, Budd proceeds to educate the Sultan and his harem. The teachers are four "school-ma'ams from the land of the cerebellum," and they are backed up by another Bostonian, Pamela Frances Jackson, judge-advocate and female reformer. Ki-Ram, biologically acquisitive, attempts to add Miss Jackson to his harem, but she is busy inciting Ki-Ram's numerous wives to sue for divorce. The complications are doubled for the Sultan by the unendurable faithfulness of his first wife, Galula: "Think of the homeliest woman you ever saw; multiply her unloveliness by two, and you will have Galula."

The Sultan's only solace is found in the cocktail, an American joy which follows the flag. When Ki-Ram's problems crowd, he makes for the nearest "life-saving station." The hit song of the play was R-E-M-O-R-S-E sung by Ki-Ram:

> The cocktail is a pleasant drink;
> It's mild and harmless—I don't think.
> When you've had one, you call for two,
> And then you don't care what you do.
> Last night I hoisted twenty-three
> Of those arrangements into me.
> My wealth increased, I swelled with pride,
> I was pickled, primed, and ossified;
> But R-E-M-O-R-S-E!
> The water wagon is the place for me.
> I think that somewhere in the game
> I wept and told my real name.
> At four I sought my whirling bed;
> At eight I woke with such a head!
> It is no time for mirth and laughter,
> The cold, gray dawn of the morning after.
> I wanted to pay for ev'ry round;
> I talked on subjects most profound;
> When all my woes I analyzed,
> The barkeep softly sympathized.
> The world was one kaleidoscope
> Of purple bliss, transcendent hope.
> But now I'm feeling mighty blue—
> Three cheers for the W.C.T.U.!
> R-E-M-O-R-S-E!
> Those dry Martinis did the work for me;
> Last night at twelve I felt immense,
> Today I feel like thirty cents.
> My eyes are bleared, my coppers hot,
> I'll try to eat, but I cannot.
> It is no time for mirth and laughter,
> The cold, gray dawn of the morning after.
>   (311-12)

The cocktail was temporary solace, but it soon added to the woes of Ki-Ram a legion of rats: "blue ones with acetylene eyes." The pitiful Sultan then feels the lash of the judge-advocate who enters the scene "wearing a Portia cap and gown, and very much on her official dignity."

PAMELA. Governor Ki-Ram!

KI-RAM. Oh-h! Here she is again. I don't believe I'm going to like her very well.

PAMELA. I have granted divorces to seven of your wives.

KI-RAM. Oh, very well!

PAMELA. The court holds that you may keep *one.*

KI-RAM. *One!* Oh, say, Judge, let me keep two; now, don't be stingy. Let me keep two little ones instead of one big one (316-17).

Ki-Ram learns that each of his divorced wives is entitled to one-half of his income. This financial problem results in Ki-Ram's incarceration and in the realization that he "loved not wisely, but too often." He plots with his secretary, Hadji, to marry off his divorced wives to remove the burden of owing them four times his income in alimony. The entanglement is finally resolved by a United States Supreme Court order reinstating Ki-Ram to all the perquisites of office, including the joyful power of deporting Pamela Frances Jackson, judge-advocate, back to Boston.

The play moves at a rapid and zany pace. The lyrics lack the zestful lilt and nimbleness of Gilbert's lines, but the spoof is neatly executed, and the imperialistic policies of the United States are scored with telling wit.[15] Ki-Ram is a dancing-tongued clown who delights with his tart observations, helpless innocence, and colorful language. The playgoer hoped for a helping of Ade's famous slang and got it. "You don't seem to understand," Ki-Ram says to Hadji. "This plan of mine is intended to get *me* out of trouble. It's not any wide-spread, benevolent undertaking of a Carnegie character. It's simply a very foxy plan by which your uncle Ki-Ram is going to give the loud, metallic ha-ha to Hasty Helen" (336).

The play has a brassy gusto and supplied the actors with opportunities for hilarious stage business. The brilliance of the costumes; the beauty of the girls; the provocative satire on politics, diplomacy, and the military; some fairly snappy lyrics;

and a crisp, fast-moving dialogue—all these easily carried a plotless hodgepodge of clean, wholesome fun. The play, fresh and compelling, was a box-office hit. In attempting an explanation of his success, Ade wrote: "Undoubtedly the 'Sultan' has endured on Broadway because it possesses a straggling few of the virtues exemplified in the remarkable librettos written by Mr. Gilbert."[16]

The press was kind. The reviews agreed that the play produced a continuous roar of laughter and applause. The New York *Sun's* critic hit the keynote of the play's reviews: "There was no possible question of the popular success of the production. Wise men may go about to-day and shake their heads. They may declare that the librettist violated the probabilities, the proprieties, the unities, and the Code Napoleon. They may assert that the composer could not differentiate between counterpoint and counterpanes; but they cannot state that 'The Sultan of Sulu' did not delight last night's audience, unless they put truth at the bottom of a well."

Life's James S. Metcalfe wrote the most sensitive analysis of the play and the most valid assessment of Ade's achievement: "Ade has managed to inject some originality into the hackneyed musical comedy idea. . . . Its humor is fresh and clean, and its special value lies in the promise it gives of a libretto-writer who may have brains to get away from the set lines of a form of entertainment which has been done almost to death. . . . 'The Sultan of Sulu' is considerably better than most of its kind."[17]

"Ingenious . . . bright . . . sparkling," admired *The Theatre*.[18] And so *The Sultan of Sulu* and George Ade, playwright, were propitiously launched.

IV A Ripe Bermuda

Peggy from Paris succeeded *The Sultan of Sulu* at Wallack's Theater on September 10, 1903, but it perished after a mediocre run of eighty-five performances. The play has the taste of a potboiler tossed together in a few weeks. Ade was stoking up his literary fires, and, instead of sparks, they were shooting forth royalties. He was still writing fables for the syndicate; *The Sultan of Sulu* was a hit on the road; and a new play, *The County Chairman*, opened in Chicago to thunderous applause.

Peggy from Paris opens with a rustic gathering in the Commercial Hotel of Hickory Crick, Illinois. The Honorable Jabez

Flanders, local politician and orator extraordinary, announces: "We are here to raise funds, or, as you might say, money, for that noble organization, the Hickory Crick-Richard-Harding-Davis-Literary-Club and Social Circle."[19] Listening are the fair daughters of Hickory Crick, a chorus of squirming children, and selected rural characters. Talk soon turns to Peggy Plummer, and the audience learns that Peggy was about to enter Galesburg Normal School when a violent hail storm destroyed forty acres of her father's oats, forty acres of corn, and burned the barn to the ground. Peggy's plans dissolved with the hail stones. Fortunately, Mrs. Greenfield of "Peory" had taken a shine to Peggy on a visit to Hickory Crick. She offered to take the poor girl as her companion on a trip to Paris. This resulted in six years of Parisian residence for Peggy, and she has just returned to the United States to take an operatic role in a Chicago theater. After a modest success singing in Paris, Peggy has returned to America as Fleurette Caramelle, the sensational Parisian soprano. The continental charms of Fleurette Caramelle have melted Chicago. As entrepreneur Montague Fish points out: "Anyone who expects to be popular in this country should arrange it so as to be born in Europe" (12).

Her father, Captain Alonzo Plummer, the epitome of Hickory Crick values, is on his way to visit Peggy. Alonzo locates his daughter, who protects her career by insisting that she is Mademoiselle Fleurette. She passes off her German maid, blowsy Sophie Blatz, as Peggy Plummer to the cruel and comic befuddlement of her father. The suspicious bewilderment of Alonzo becomes the central conflict of the play, but it is sketchily developed. He suspects that Fleurette is Peggy, and, to be near her, he substitutes for the butler at the biggest blowout of the operatic season. To calm the old man's suspicion, Sophie Blatz hires a tattooist and has him counterfeit a strawberry mole that breaks the monotony of Peggy's back. Alonzo's tenuous conviction that Fleurette is Peggy is shaken by this artful deception, but the instincts of a father are too strong even for this evidence.

The play is riddled with specialty numbers and a hodgepodge of comic asides:

Plummer. (Entering C. with dog under his arm) The Commander of the G.A.R.—taking care of a dog.

Fish. You servants will have to keep out of here.

Plummer. Servants? I'll have you to understand that I'm Chief of the Fire Department, and I'm here to look after my daughter.

Fish. Which one?

Plummer. Peggy.

Fish. Don't worry about her; I have seen her, she's safe anywhere.

Plummer. (Approaches him confidentially) About six years ago in Hickory Crick—

Fish. Wait! Is this a *proper* story?

Plummer. Yes, sir.

Fish. Then I don't care to hear it at all.

Plummer. (*As he exits*) I forgot I was in society (20).

The pressure on Peggy begins to tell, for she is a good, sweet, loving American girl at heart; and the spectacle of her father's humiliation disturbs her. In spite of losing fortune, fame, adoration, and Chicago, she blurts out the truth. "I stood it as long as I could. An American girl can't be any other kind of a girl." Just before the finale Peggy turns to the audience with tears in her eyes and proclaims: "From European shams and imitations, spare us, if you were born in Illinois don't try to come from Paris."

Peggy from Paris had only half the run of *The Sultan of Sulu,* and it earned far less than half the critical praise. The critics enjoyed, however, the opening pageant of rustics, a device that was to become a highly regarded convention in the Ade plays that were to follow. In *Peggy from Paris* the audience met Jim Peasely, a garrulous whistle-stop telegrapher; Alonzo Plummer, inveterate town official; Jabez Flanders, loquacious village politician; Walt Quackenbush, country philosopher of the commonplace; Lem Harvey, town vagrant; Mrs. Homer Ketcham, bubbling busybody; and Alexander Nerveen, drugstore dandy. The pageant sparkled with miniatures that had the tang of caricature and the tone of truth. For a moment the audience was refreshed by a breeze from the *Fables,* but its hope died with the first act and turned to ashes by the end of the second.

To vivify a vapid plot, Ade injected overdoses of slang. Gone was the comparatively high tone of *The Sultan of Sulu,* and words like "Whillykazoozle" abound. This passage indicates how he bombed the audience with slang:

Reginald. As I started to tell you—I goes up to the shack, pushes the zing-zing and out comes a pale gazook with a bunch of Virginia creepers in front of each listener.

Fish. I beg pardon.

Reginald. I say, I drilled up to the hut—push the white bean and out comes a guy and a Mardi-Gras makeup, with a fire escape on each side of his lip (12-13).

The main plot is all but obscured by the specialty numbers and comic vignettes strewn upon the stage. Among these are the story of the girl who walked in her sleep and who was given carfare by her mother before bedtime; and the story of Sophie Blatz's lost love is explained by the song "Henny and his Bassoon."

The lyrics of *Peggy* are pedestrian; the book is feeble; and the music by William Loraine was reportedly uninspired. The temptation is to turn the words of Reginald against his creator: "I hate to throw the harpoon into a nice man with ivy all over his face, but I think this comic opera of yours is a large ripe Bermuda" (14).

The press was basically in agreement with Reggie's summation. Critical praise was largely confined to enthusiasm for the pageant. "It is a comic opera that is nearly devoid of prettiness," wrote Alan Dale in the New York *American*. "The new affair is as arid as the Sahara Desert, as irritating as an African sandstorm. It is without vegetation. It has no shade. . . . New York is very spoiled. It is so accustomed to rot manufactured here for it that it can see no great value in the provincial article." Dale assaulted *Peggy from Paris* as "dull," "ineffective," "pointless." He dismissed Loraine's score as a brunette might pluck a blonde hair from an escort's shoulder: "The music of 'Peggy' might be anybody from anywhere. It is certainly light as thistledown. In fact, it is more like thistledown than music."

The New York *Sun*'s reviewer scoffed: "There is no use of unloading the crushing burden of serious consideration on this production. A single weighty thought would break its back."

Ade was guilty of hacking out the musical claptrap that both he and the critics abhorred. His reputation was redeemed, however, by *The County Chairman*, which succeeded *Peggy* at Wallack's and was soon playing to STANDING ROOM ONLY crowds.

CHAPTER 5

The Baron of Broadway

> Augustus Thomas introduced me at The
> Lambs . . . and said there had been some
> controversy as to whether I was a playwright
> or a farmer. He said he had investigated and
> learned that in Indiana I was regarded as a
> playwright and in New York City I was
> known as a farmer.
>
> —"How to Live in the Country"

AFTER MAKING three musical plays, Ade tried his hand at straight comedy and wrote the two outstanding hits of his career. *The County Chairman* and *The College Widow* marked the zenith of Ade's achievement and popularity as a playwright. Never again was he to ride so high or to hear America roar his praises so loudly.

I *Politics*

The County Chairman charmed New Yorkers for 237 nights before it closed for the season on June 4, 1904. It reopened in September for an additional forty-four performances before it went on the road where it was popular for several years.

Ade wrote his first non-musical comedy in about one-fourth the time that he needed for his musical plays. He decided to write this one without slang, and he delighted in his task. From the glitter and tinsel of song, dance, and gusty patter, it was a relief to fill the stage with sun bonnets, hickory shirts, blue jeans, and gingham dresses. The pageantry begun in *Peggy from Paris* became a major feature in *The County Chairman*. A notable stream of character types flooded the stage in a profusion that Ade was unable to control. The success of his rustic pageant took Broadway by storm. Ade's brilliant array of types

were marshalled from the fables, imagination, and a lucky
accident or two:

> While I was incubating the play I had been the guest, in Vicks-
> burg, Mississippi, of Harris Dickson, author of the "Old Reliable"
> yarns and many other entertaining stories of Southern atmos-
> phere. He showed me around his home town and, among other
> points of interest connected with the famous siege directed by
> Gen. Grant, we visited the old Court House where some of the
> shells, sent over by Union gunners, were still imbedded in the
> walls. In the lobby of the Court House was a bulletin board
> bearing the names of citizens who were delinquent in their
> taxes. Perhaps because I have always been interested in names
> I read the list as posted on the board and found that it was a
> grand roster of good old Anglo-Saxon names. I secured a copy
> and, later, when I was ready to devise names for all of the
> undiluted American "types" to be found in Antioch, scene of
> The County Chairman, I brought out the names of the tax
> delinquents and found all of the Hacklers, Rigbys, Wheelers,
> Tollivers, Watsons and others needed for a cast which would seem
> authentic and homegrown.[1]

During the casting of the play, Ade learned that Willis
Sweatnam, the old-time minstrelman, was living on the free
lunch. He rewrote a part for Sweatnam, who repaid the kindness
by becoming the hit of the play.

Tumbling onstage like a fall of autumn leaves, Ade's people
bustled with activity:

> I had the colored man bring in a basket of eggs, the hired
> man came in riding a bicycle, the girl from the boarding-house
> with a wringer to be repaired, the traveling man with the model
> of a patent windmill, the politician a poll-book that needed
> verifying, the boy a fish-pole and a string of fish, the sweet
> young heroine a basket of wild flowers, the station agent the
> mail bag, and so on throughout the play.[2]

The first scene opens in front of Vance Jimmison's general
store on the main street of Antioch, the seat of Jefferson County.
The sound of a harmonica wafts across the lazy street and within
a few minutes about thirty characters gather. The talk is casual,
countrified, and tends to politics and pleasantry until the advent
of Jefferson Briscoe, store-porch orator. Briscoe does little to
advance the plot, but he kicks off the first of the comic vignettes
characteristic of Ade's dramatic technique.

BRISCOE. (*Has been sitting on porch L. of doorway, reading paper, now rises, crumpling paper, excited*) Well, if that ain't enough to make a man cuss! (*On front porch.*) Palaverin' an' wastin' words. There's only one way, gentleman—(*Slapping fist in hand*)—to git any satisfaction out of Great Britain, an' that's to fight 'em!

CLEAVER. What's the matter now, Jeff?

BRISCOE. Why, this Behrin' Sea business. It's come up ag'in and, as usual, they're talkin' compromise and arbitration. Arb'tration nothin'. We've licked 'em twice an', sure as my name's Jefferson Briscoe, we'll have to do it again!

UNCLE ECK. Oh, Jeff!

BRISCOE. (*Coming down from porch to c.*) Well?

UNCLE ECK. Where *is* this Behrin' Sea?

BRISCOE. (*Hesitates a moment*) Don't make no difference where it is. (*A general titter from others.*) The question is, air we, the greatest and most powerful nation on earth, goin' to set back an' be bully-ragged an' horn-swoggled by some Jim Crow island that looks, by ginger, like a freckle on the ocean! (CHUB *rushes on*) If they had any backbone at Washington—

CHUB. Say, Jeff, she's comin' an' she's got blood in her eye! (*All start nervously.*)

BRISCOE. (*Anxiously, looking off R.I.*) I—I don't want to have no words with her here, before a crowd of men. (*Hurries off*)[3]

Mrs. Briscoe enters the scene with the bustle and ire of her prototype, Mrs. Rip Van Winkle. A classic scold, she berates the loafers and makes a public statement concerning the contemptibleness of her lazy windbag of a husband.

As the play advances the pageant keeps pace: Amos Whitney rides up to the general store on an old-fashioned high bicycle; Chick Elzey, a pretty little orphan girl sidles winningly into the scene; and Judge Elias Rigby, cunning, self-seeking politician, enters to inquire about the local political convention which is deadlocked. Jupiter Pettaway, manager of the Antioch Fife and Drum Corps, baits Rigby on the absorption of Chick Elzey's inheritance in legal fees levied by the judge who is acting as her "guardeen." Sassafras Livingstone, "a touch of local color," sidles up to the judge in his ingratiating way and says: "Judge Rigby, suh, I'm foh you. People come round askin' who you all goin' to vote foh persecuting attorney. I say Judge

'Lias Rigby. No need to offeh me no money to vote for no one
else 'cause I knows who my frien's is. I say, 'I kin go to Judge
Rigby any ole time, an' git *anything* I want' " (14).

Shortly a traveling drummer, Joseph Whittaker, enters in-
quiring for Jim Hackler, the county chairman. He doesn't find
Hackler, but he does meet Lorena Watkins, milliner and town
vamp. Aside from this stage business the conversation again
turns to politics. Rigby is supported by Briscoe and several
other prominent townspeople for prosecuting attorney of Jefferson County. His chief opponent, Hackler, is backing young
Tillford Wheeler, who is in love with Lucy Rigby, the judge's
daughter. The plot is further complicated by Hackler's detesta-
tion of Rigby, and it is soon learned that Hackler is still in love
with Rigby's wife who was his childhood sweetheart.

The game of politics soon takes center stage. Hackler has uncovered Rigby's theft of his ward's inheritance, but he cannot
get his candidate's approval to use the information. Wheeler
would rather lose the election than destroy his chances with
Lucy Rigby. He agrees with Lucy that he will not attack her
father. Wheeler, however, is goaded into a row with Rigby and
breaks his promise by publicly denouncing his opponent as
"grasping, greedy, selfish—." The scene ends in a mêlée and the
second act curtain falls on a spectacular riot.

Act III opens in the shabby law office of Hackler and
Wheeler where a group of loafers discusses the county chairman's mysterious trip to Illinois. Several comic characters trip
successively upon the stage: Mrs. Briscoe adds to her termagant
role; the milliner screams into the office to sue the drummer for
breach of promise; and Sassafras Livingstone shuffles in to
pledge his support to Wheeler:

SASSAFRAS. Misteh Wheeleh, I—(*Cigar bus. during this speech
. . .*) I've been waitin' to get a chance to repoht. I've been
doin' consid'able wohk—spendin' my money freely, and I desiah
to repoht that ev'ything looks fav'able. You will cert'n'y be our
next Cong'essman.

WHEELER. I'm not running for Congress. I'm running for
Prosecuting Attorney.

SASSAFRAS. Well, whateveh you're runnin' foh, you'll be it.
By the way, Mr. Wheeleh, I've got something to show you that'll
cert'n'y inteh—intehest—please you. (*Takes envelope from pocket,
tied with shoestring.*) There it is, suh! (*Unties it and takes
tintype out.*) A tintype of T.W.

WHEELER. T.W.?

SASSAFRAS. (*Holds tintype out to him, face turned partly away L.*) Tillford Wheeler Livingstone. Yes, suh! Smahtest boy you eveh saw. (WHEELER *rises, smiling . . .*) Fo' weeks old an' knows who's runnin' foh office. I'm teachin' him to say, "Hurrah foh Tillford Wheeleh." Of course, it don't sound much like anything unless you're familiah with the language used by a child of that age—(*Looks round at chair; finds* WHEELER *gone. Looks round for him rising, sees him back of table, smiles.*) I missed your presence.

WHEELER. Look here, Sassafras, I was talking to Doc. McLain the other night and he tells me that this new baby of yours is a girl.

SASSAFRAS. A girl?

WHEELER. That's what he says, and he ought to know.

SASSAFRAS. (*Hesitates, smiles feebly*) Well, yes, suh, that's right. The doctoh is right. It's a gihl.

WHEELER. Well, how can a girl be named Tillford?

SASSAFRAS. Who said anything about Tillford?

WHEELER. You did.

SASSAFRAS. Tillford? I said 'at baby's name was Tilly—Tilly, suh. We sometimes call it Tillford for short—when we's in a hurry—but its regulah name is Tilly. Tilly is she for Tillford—that's what we calls it. Named after you, suh. (WHEELER *convulsed with laughter.*)

WHEELER. (*Laughing, takes coin from pocket and gives it to* SASSAFRAS) Well, here's a half dollar, anyway. You buy something for the infant.

SASSAFRAS. (*Takes it*) Yes, suh. I'll buy some peppehmint candy (85-87).

Lucy Rigby enters in fury to confront Hackler about a report that he intends to denounce her father as a thief. Wheeler backs Lucy but to no avail. Hackler is adamant that "all's fair in love—an' war—an' politics." Rigby then warns Hackler not to print the story. Finding threats worthless, he makes a sentimental appeal to their boyhood friendship. Hackler's retort reveals the source of his hatred for Rigby:

You know that when a man keeps after another man, the way I've kept after you, it's something besides politics. Do you remember that morning twenty years ago, the home company went away—the crowd at the depot—and Mary Leonard there to tell us good-bye, both of us? Me and you stood on the platform and waved to her as far as we could see. I had the inside track that day, and you knew it by the way she acted. When we got into camp at Maysville, you was made orderly sergeant—you handled the mails both ways. That was when her letters stopped comin' to me and my letters stopped goin' to her. . . . She thought I'd forgotten her, off there at the front. I didn't suspect—you went home on a furlough—sickness. That was your long suit. An' she, for some reason, God knows what, up and married you. I heard about it—that's why I reenlisted in the field. Didn't come back till it was all over, and then I heard it all. How Mary Leonard wrote to me an' waited—an' wrote to me an' waited—until she was too proud to write again. Then I came home and little Lucy was three months old, an' I didn't dare let on or say a word. An' I ain't—from that day to this. But I've been after you every minute. You tricked me out of the only woman I ever cared for. You're the only man on earth I hate clean through—an' I've got you where I want you—(96-97).

At this moment Mary Rigby enters to beg Hackler not to humiliate Lucy and her. After a struggle, Hackler destroys the story, and the curtain of the third act falls.

The final act solves all: Wheeler wins the election and Lucy; Hackler makes a public announcement that Rigby has located three thousand dollars of his ward's inheritance. Rigby is "sandbagged" and the stage erupts in spectacular hubbub. Crowds cheer; bands blare; Sassafras breaks into a buck dance. Off to one side Mary Rigby stands sadly by her dejected husband, and Jim Hackler, the county chairman, stares hopelessly at the woman he still loves.

The critics were as effusive as the public was enthusiastic. But Howells grumbled about the play in a letter to H. B. Fuller: "I think Ade's play not good enough for him. It is a pity; I can't understand how so absolute a talent could do such a comparative thing. He had a great chance, in the *County Chairman,* but he has missed its greatness."[4] Howells saw realism fall before the glow of romance once again, and, having hoped so much of Ade, the sight was doubly unpleasant. Actually, Howells had been too generous in his estimate of Ade's capabilities. Ade had a rare talent for realistic observation, but he was totally lacking in the mental discipline required to warp this talent into the austerely selective channel of realism. Despicable though Rigby is, one is neither antagonistic to his character nor repulsed by his sin. He is a naughty puppet. Ade could not have made him otherwise; he had neither the ability nor the desire.

It is now difficult to appreciate the freshness of *The County Chairman,* for it bristles with original characters destined to become stereotypes. But Ade had created a gallery of characters never before seen on the American stage, but to be seen frequently after 1904. The critics were quick to see Ade's contribution and hailed him for his realism, Howells notwithstanding. The New York *Daily Tribune* extolled the play for its "thread of almost photographic realism." The *World* found it "typically American and truly amusing." The *Evening Sun* claimed for Ade "a triumph in the matter of characterization." The *Herald* praised the play for its real and human characterizations that must be recognized even by "hustling and self-centered Broadway."

Sweatnam's success was especially noted. James S. Metcalfe wrote:

> In Mr. George Ade's "The County Chariman" we have in the Sassafras Livingstone of Mr. Willis P. Sweatnam, a veteran minstrel, a piece of character-acting well worthy of notice as an artistic accomplishment. It is a broad characterization, to be sure, but in its drawing and its truth to nature it deserves to rank with the depiction of more complicated individualities. Behind the unusually faithful external delineation of the character, we see the working of the negro mind, with its strong appreciation of creature comforts and its would-be extremely artful methods for obtaining them.[5]

Howells reviewed *The County Chairman* for *Harper's Weekly* and expressed the misgiving that the stage "had prevailed too much with the caustic wit" of Ade, and that

> he [Ade] had done what it wished him to do, rather than what he wished himself to do. There was a whistling and a too opportune boy who had come out of the property-room, and there was a troop of Indiana villagers who had been translated from a comic-opera chorus for the purpose they were put to. The purpose was such as sopranos and contraltos are never put to in the Middle West, as I recall it; for women take no part in politics there, though they sometimes do so at the East in emulation of Englishwomen politicians. In democracies, women stay

at home during political campaigns, quite as much as if the campaigns were military, and the Middle West is distinctly a democracy in this respect. There is indeed one fine instant in which the youth of both sexes mingle in Mr. Ade's play, not only probably, but inevitably, and all flock to see the five-ten express come in, and enjoy the one excitement of their forty-eight hour day. That is like a touch in some of the *Fables*, and there is a preciously worthless darky in the piece, who is like a vision of the real thing from *Pink Marsh*.[6]

The County Chairman has been largely ignored in histories of American drama. It is the worthiest of Ade's plays and deserves more than the cursory notices it has received in the few histories that have deigned to notice Ade at all. One scholar has said of this play: "In many respects this is the finest play on the subject yet to come out of the American theatre."[7] The same judgment can be made of Ade's next play, *The College Widow*.

II   *Football*

Before *The County Chairman* had completed its run at Wallack's, *The College Widow* opened at the Garden Theater on September 20, 1904. It was like a comet following a meteor. *The County Chairman* was one of the box-office hits of its season, but *The College Widow* was one of the smash hits of its decade. The brilliantly staged, ebullient comedy grossed two million dollars for its producers, and it turned George Ade into a literary tycoon.

The new play ran for 278 performances and enjoyed years of success on the road. While *The College Widow* was playing to Standing Room Only crowds, *The County Chairman* completed its 222nd performance and was succeeded by *The Sho-Gun*, Ade's fourth musical comedy.

Written in a burst of enthusiasm during the first three weeks of his residence at "Hazelden," his luxurious country estate in Indiana, *The College Widow* reached its majority at birth: it went from pen to production without revision.

In a letter to Everett Watkins of the Indianapolis *Star*, Ade wrote:

As I look back to 1905, I realize that I was either very courageous and far-sighted or else very foolhardy. I wanted to write a play dealing with college life and football. No play dealing with those two subjects had ever been produced on the American stage. Henry W. Savage, who had been producing my plays, and many other wise people connected with the theater were of the opinion that the general playgoing public was not keenly interested in under-graduates or college athletics. I thought they might be if we treated the college students as human beings instead of little tin gods and produced a comedy instead of a melodrama.

I did not make the mistake of picking out a big school, such as Harvard or Yale or Princeton. When I wrote the play I had Wabash in mind.[8] It is a sectarian school for men in a fairly small city and small enough to have its local characters and a provincial coloring. I tried to put into the play a lot of interesting "types" and evidently I succeeded. I wrote the play in three weeks about mid-summer in 1905 [*sic*] and it went into rehearsal in New York about August first.

Strangely enough, my newspaper and theatrical friends who attended rehearsals did not show any enthusiasm for the play. I felt in my bones that they thought it was all about something in which most people were not greatly interested. We went down to Washington for a try-out week very early in September. The opening was at the Columbia Theater. Everybody connected with the enterprise was very dubious and apprehensive. We had attended so many rehearsals during which the lines were spoken to empty benches that the dialogue seemed to have lost all sense and flavor.

I remember that on the afternoon of the opening, some of my fraternity brothers came to me and asked me to attend a reception in my honor after the opening performance. I told them that after the opening performance, I might be up in my room hiding under the bed or else floating in the Potomac River. There is no other terror so extreme as that surrounding a "first night". We had about two-thirds of a house. Congress was not in session and the weather was rather warm. The curtain went up and I began to pace up and down the strip of carpet back of the parquette.

The first act was supposed to introduce the characters and start the story, but it was not supposed to contain much comedy. My first happy surprise came when the people began to laugh and applaud during the first act. I felt encouraged. The second act went with a bang and was followed by a lot of applause. The third act, if I do say so myself, was a knock-out. It was a very short act dealing with all the thrills of a big football game. There was plenty of action and cheering and people rushing in and out of the main entrance to the playing field, all in a fine frenzy. The climax was the touchdown and the appearance of the players and their friends holding the hero aloft.

Well, after the third act, I had to go before the curtain and make a speech. Just at my right, as I stood on the edge of the stage, was a box containing Admiral and Mrs. Dewey and General and Mrs. Fred Grant. I thanked the audience and I said I hoped their applause was sincere. Admiral Dewey stood up in his box and said, "George, it's alright"! I saluted him and said, "Admiral, God bless you for them kind words"!

Yes, the play was a hit in Washington and a hit when we opened up the Garden Theater in New York a week later. We didn't have to change any of the lines or do any revising. The play remained at the Garden until the following summer and next year it was being played by three companies. It turned out to be my meal ticket.[9]

The elaborate sets used in *The College Widow* were in part responsible for the spectacular success of the play. In a letter to Ade, a member of a road company wrote: "In moving the production to Washington, we used two sixty foot baggage cars, and to put it mildly we utilized every inch of space, packing therein the campus of Atwater, the gymnasium, the foot ball stadium, and the hotel."[10] The set for the third act was a masterpiece of design. The reviewer for *Munsey's Magazine* described it:

At the Garden Theater, where "The College Widow" lifts itself above every other attraction of the present New York season by having scored the longest run, the most striking feature of the scenic hinterland is the platform for the spectators of the football game. It is built against the rear wall, which separates the theater from the big auditorium of Madison Square Garden. In the great scene of the third act some dozen or more "supers" seat themselves on the lofty structure, which from the front, takes on the appearance of a section of the grand stand. They are quite out of reach of the prompter, and there is such an uproar on the stage that no cues can be heard. George Marion, the stage manager, came to the rescue with an electrical device and a series of sign-boards resembling nothing so much as the strips affixed to the front platforms of the Broadway trolley-cars to inform the public whether those palatial vehicles go to Murray Street or Bowling Green.

The sign-boards are kept on the edge platform, out of sight of the audience, and ranged in a consecutive pack like a calendar. The first bears the single word "Bingham," the second, "Atwater," and so on, to denote yells the supers are to emit when each is displayed by the man who holds them up. His motions, in turn, are guided by three small electric bulbs at his left, one red, another white, the third blue. The flashing of the red means "make ready"; the white, "yell"; the blue, "quit."

The supers receive fifty cents a performance, and are recruited from all walks of life.[11]

The 1904-5 dramatic season was immensely kind to George Ade. Never again was he to equal the immense financial rewards gleaned in this period. *The College Widow* and *The Sho-Gun* twinkled nightly on Broadway; *The County Chairman* was still pulling capacity crowds on the road; and, to meet the demand for *The College Widow*, two traveling companies had to be formed. During most of this season Ade collected five thousand dollars a week.

The College Widow makes use of a classic formula: the plucky underdog that comes through. Atwater College doesn't stand a chance against Bingham's juggernaut football squad. Only a miracle can save Atwater from certain defeat, and the first act opens with the usual Ade pageant: disconsolate collegians, the coach, members of the squad, townsfolk, faculty, and campus characters make the stage groan.

The first scene is the campus in front of the main building of Atwater. The time: afternoon early in the first month of the fall term. On stage are "Silent" Murphy, the newly recruited center rush of whom it is reported: "This fellow can throw a horse. . . . I saw him down at Springfield, workin' in a foundry, and I convinced him that he needed a college education"; Flora Wiggins, a prominent waitress whose mother runs a collegiate boardinghouse: "I've met so many college comedians I ain't got a laugh left in my system"; Mrs. Primley Dalzelle, a young widow turned professional chaperone whose principal pursuit is the male student; the Honorable Elam Hicks of Squantamville, member of the state senate who admonishes his son before leaving him at Atwater: "And don't you learn to play no ukelele—that'll ruin any young man"; Jane Witherspoon, the college widow, of whom Bessie Tanner, muscle-bound girl athlete says: "She's been wearing somebody's college pin for the last five years. Her shirtwaists are so full of holes that they look like openwork"; Copernicus Talbot, pedantic tutor; Daniel Tibbits, suspicious, mustachioed town marshal; Hiram Bolton,

D.D., LL.D., philanthropic philistine, proud of being a captain of industry; Peter Witherspoon, Woodrow Wilson-like president of Atwater College; and other character types.

The play greatly relies, as do most of Ade's plays, on the gem-like vignettes which carry much of the laughter and most of the satire. In Act I Billy Bolton meets his father on the campus of Atwater where that great industrialist is visiting his old friend, Peter Witherspoon. Billy is scheduled to enter Bingham College, Atwater's bitter rival, and his father is in the process of concluding negotiations for a tutor:

BOLTON. (*Offering him cigar, which he refuses*) Mr. Talbot, no need wastin' much talk on this deal. The pay's satisfactory—you know what you've got to do—take him over to Bingham and whenever he can spare any time from football, you make him study a little.

TALBOT. What class does he enter?

BOLTON. (*Lights a match*) Well, he's been a freshman for three years out west. He's gettin' used to it now. I s'pose we'd better make him a freshman.

TALBOT. What course, may I inquire?

BOLTON. I don't care what he takes so it ain't botany. Of all the idiotic—Here, I'll tell you about my own case. Over thirty years ago I went to Bingham College to please my mother. I lasted till the Spring term. Then a long whiskered professor came to me with a common, ornery dandelion, and says, "I want you to find out the scientific name of this." I says, "I don't care a continental *what* the scientific name is. I'm a full grown man and I don't propose to waste my time pickin' dandelions to pieces." So they fired me.

TALBOT. Really?

BOLTON. (*Leaning on fence*) I went out west—joined a surveyin' gang—got into the railroad business. Well, I've always been so grateful to Bingham College for savin' me from a professional career that I've put up three or four buildings for them.

TALBOT. I can hardly understand your position, Mr. Bolton—you are opposed to collegiate training and yet you have endowed Bingham College.

BOLTON. Oh, colleges do some good—they keep a good many light-weights out of the railroad business. But there ain't any money in a college education. (*Coming to* TALBOT.) Look at Pete

Witherspoon. He was a smart boy—workin' now for three thousand dollars a year.

TALBOT.   Ah, but the triumphs of scholarship!

BOLTON.   What are they? The best he's got is a Ph.D. and I'm a D.D., LL.D.—clean up half a million a year besides. Your college presidents don't get that much.[12]

Billy Bolton never gets to Bingham College. Billy, an All-American halfback, is shanghaied by Coach Larrabee who is the current interest of Jane Witherspoon, the college widow. Larrabee cajoles Jane into vamping Billy. Once the charms of the widow have drugged the star halfback, he is Atwater's. While his father is in Europe, Billy shrugs off Bingham College and charts its defeat on the gridiron to please Jane. The machinations of the coach, the widow, and various members of the football squad fill the second act; and, before the curtain falls, Billy is irrevocably committed to the destruction of his father's alma mater.

The big game fills the spectacular third act. Booming with fight songs, cheers, and band music; opulent with the tints and lighting of autumn; and ablaze with uniforms, Indian blankets, and cherry and white pennants, the stage is a carnival of collegiate color and excitement.

The score at the end of the first half is 6-0 in favor of Bingham College. When Atwater runs onto the field for the second half, the team shows the strain: suits are heavily soiled, faces are streaked with perspiration. The team is a rough, tough, desperate squad. The tension in the stands is at its highest pitch. Jane tells her father: "Father, if we lose this game, I'll blame you! You compelled those poor boys to attend recitations when they should have been practicing!"

Billy Bolton plays his heart out, even though Bingham has selected him for execution. The mêlée becomes so heated that President Witherspoon is painfully upset: "And Atwater was founded to foster the Presbyterian faith! What would John Calvin say to this?"

In the last quarter Bingham still leads by a touchdown. Tom Pearson, the right tackle, is carried, injured, from the field. The Atwater student body starts a chant for Billy. He responds and threatens Bingham's lead. The possibility of a touchdown infects the throng. At this crucial moment Hiram Bolton bustles into the stadium livid with anger. Fortunately Jane thinks quickly, faints into his arms, and gives the friends of Atwater College time to organize a sortie against the elder Bolton and to deport him from the stadium. At this point the cries of "Hold 'em" become louder and more frantic. A "sudden pandemonium of noise—cheers—howls—horn-tooting" assails the audience. Larrabee enters in despair:

LARRABEE. Boys, we're done for!

PEARSON and MCGOWAN. What?

LARRABEE. Within two yards of the line and goin' through us like paper!

MCGOWAN. Oh, hell!

PEARSON. Same here!

BESSIE. Jack, Jack Larrabee, come on—come back! Hurrah!

ALL THREE. (*Starting*) Bolton!

BESSIE. They had it right up against the line—through—through! (*Gesture to indicate repeated charges and gains.*) Half a minute to play. I was crying—I was crying!

LARRABEE. (*Shaking her*) Oh, for heaven's sake!

BESSIE. They started to buck center!

OTHERS. (*Eagerly*) Yes! Yes!

BESSIE. A fumble! (*Exclamations by three.*) Bolton—through like a flash—picked up the ball—down the field!

LARRABEE, MCGOWAN, and PEARSON. What!

BESSIE. He went through 'em—over 'em—like a streak of lightnin'—right between the posts!

LARRABEE. A touchdown?

BESSIE. Don't you hear that noise? (*She rushes off c., followed by Larrabee. Pearson starts, greatly excited, and is forcibly held by McGowan.*)

PEARSON. Let me go, Matty!

MCGOWAN. Sit down, Tommy, old pal! I'll take a peek. (*He climbs on top of porch on training quarters near gate so that he can look over. The uproar dies down.*) Bolton goin' to kick!

PEARSON. How is he?

MCGOWAN. A little wobbly, but I guess—(*pause*) He's walking up.

PEARSON. Wish I hadn't forgotten how to pray!

MCGOWAN. Oh-h-h! False alarm! He's walkin' back again.

PEARSON. Right against the wind, too!

(A momentary pause—then terrific cheering and Atwater yell. MCGOWAN leaps to ground and does a wild dance. PEARSON waves crutches. . . . The noise outside . . . intense and growing as the crowd come from the field. Billy, carried on shoulders, is brought c., surrounded by everybody. . . . As many extra people as can be used—girls, students, professors. Flags waving, hats in the air. Probably the first curtain should be Billy, battered and dirty, held aloft at c. On curtain everybody off except Jane. The stage is in upset condition, fences down, hats strewn about. The crowd has moved off L. Jane looking off L., then sinks to bench for "good cry." (89-91.)

Jane, having fallen in love with Billy Bolton, is now faced with the cheapness of her deception as the curtain falls on Act III. The last act soothes the exhausted audience with a gentle pageant in front of the Grand Hotel. Students lounge in collegiate garb and sing school songs on the porch while the hotel windows blossom with lovely town girls. The festive pageant fills the street, and the time for the comic vignettes has again arrived. Billy faces his father who admiringly relents after screaming at his son: "You're a hell of a Baptist!" Jane confesses her duplicity; Billy proposes; and the play ends in jubilee.

The College Widow was a *tour de force* that romped barefoot over a delighted Broadway audience. The satire is delicious. All the pretentious balloons of college athletics are punctured; pedantry withers under laughter; and parvenu arrogance is painlessly eviscerated. The contrast of Witherspoon and Talbot with the elder Bolton and the cretinish collegians epitomized in "Silent" Murphy and Bub Hicks hold up to genial laughter the extremes found in the small-town American college. Ade's preoccupation with absurd rural types was a minor chapter in the "Revolt from the Village" movement.

The College Widow was acclaimed for its vivid characters and the brilliant, breathless, happily-staged carnage of Act III. The audience literally cheered the play. George Marion, the stage director, wrote: "At the opening of the College Widow . . . the audience kept up the applause at the finish of the third act until the curtain arose on the fourth act a matter of some twelve to fifteen minutes."[13]

All of the reviews commended the magnificent staging and execution of the third act: "It was a Whangdoodle Walloper of a scene," slanged the *Evening Journal*. "The house has a spasm and goes straight up into the ether," said the *Sun*. The reputatation of George Ade was at its zenith, and Indiana almost burst with pride.[14]

The critics were delighted with the play. The New York *American* wrote: "Once again genuine humor of dialogue and of character was successfully pitted against the drool and drivel of dialect rubbish." "A tumult of delight," proclaimed the New York *Mail*. "A real, old-fashioned, howling success," roared the *Morning World*. "Shriekingly funny," echoed the *Evening World*. The *Telegraph* said: "Every line . . . is a hit. Every situation is humorous. It is a true comedy. . . . Mr. Ade has written one of the best comedies . . . that has been seen in America in at least a decade. Mr. Ade . . . is the great American master of comedy." "Thoroughly satisfactory," said the *News*. "Infectious," said the *Herald*. "A great popular success," proclaimed the *Tribune*. "Phenomenal," was the judgment of the *Sun*. "A touchdown," cheered the *Evening Telegram*.

William Bullock of the *Press* wrote the most restrained review: " 'The College Widow' does not strike one as a great play, but . . . the salient point is that it catches the fancy; it holds interest from start to finish. More than once it carries the auditor close to irresponsible enthusiasm. There is a healthy, vigorous tone about 'The College Widow' that is distinctly uplifting and pleasing. The play appeals because of its naturalness; it holds attention because it is without pretense of profundity. Ade does not bother himself with any problem of the sexes; rather he chooses to give us entertaining pictures of folk like ourselves—pictures from which the shadows of carnal spirits are jealously guarded."

The play was certainly one of the great popular hits in the annals of the American stage. "One must go back to the old days of Harrigan and Hart at the Theatre Comique on lower Broadway," wrote the *Dramatic News*, "to find the time when a first-night audience rose en masse and cheered everybody from the players to the author, from the author to the producer, and from the producer to the stage manager."[15]

New York went wild over *The College Widow*. Crowds stormed the box office. Scalpers honed their knives near the Garden Theater, and Producer Savage was attacked for being in collusion with the sidewalk hawkers. Playgoers were competing to pay ten and twenty dollars for a ticket. There were frequent scuffles among speculators and legitimate customers; the box office was subjected to prodigies of invective until Savage hired two burly Negroes who stood on cabs near the theater and bellowed warnings against the hawkers. They were armed with gigantic megaphones that projected their voices more than two blocks away. The doorman refused to admit buyers of black-market tickets, and the furor and speculative profit alike soon died down to the usual whisper that will ever be overheard in the vicinity of a smash hit.

Two road companies were soon hustling through the hinterlands on one, two, and three night stands. The longest run on the road was in Chicago where *The College Widow* remained from July 31, 1905, to September 10, 1905. It could have remained indefinitely, but it was forced to leave because of other commitments. The business in Chicago was so profitable, however, that the troupe was immediately scheduled to return on March 19, 1906. It played to packed houses until May 13.

The enthusiasm was so high and constant for the play that its producer decided it would get a sterling reception in England. On April 20, 1908, *The College Widow* opened at the Adelphi Theatre in London and remained for thirty performances. Ade, Marion, and the manager of the Adelphi had strong reservations about the chances of the play, but Savage was insistent. He agreed to make one concession: a glossary of slang terms to be inserted in the program. The glossary itself was hilarious to Londoners: "Pinkest Collection of Farm Hands" was translated as "Dullest lot of creatures"; "Pin-Head" meant "A man of inferior capacity"; and "A Web-Footed Rube" was "An uncouth countryman." The harried critic of the London *Daily Express* wrote: "The conscientious man who turned trustingly to the glossary for the purpose of tracking down obscure Indiana epithets invariably found, on returning his attention to the stage, that the Widow and her slap-dash satellites had forged five or six miles ahead, and left him enveloped in a cloud of dust."

Taken as a whole, the London reviews of *The College Widow* were enthusiastic and bewildered. "Laugh? Gee-Whiz!!" said the London *Daily Mail*. "Genuine fun . . . the brightest of fare," said the *Evening News*. The *Star* found the play a "merry romp, naïve and artless and almost childish . . . the most breathless

play in town." "An anaesthetic in four acts . . . simply paralysing
. . . in the language of one of his characters—"Gee! Ain't it
fierce?" exclaimed the *Daily Express*. "The piece is brilliantly
mounted," wrote the *Standard*. "And for its astonishing vivacity,
its humour and its freshness should certainly be a great success.
It is not so much a play as a panorama and a pandemonium, but
it is capital entertainment." "Not so much a play as a whirlwind. . . . Fortunately, the result, though tempestuous, is wholly
pleasurable," said the *Evening Standard*. "An admirable evening's
entertainment, exciting, laughable, wholesome and novel," wrote
the *Financial Times*. "Every moment of it is enjoyable," said the
Times. "Quite exciting," said the *Daily Mirror*. "There is nothing
else to compare with it in life, movement, bustle, and infectious
enthusiasm," said the *Daily Telegraph*. "Jolly good fun," cheered
Punch. "If anybody says it isn't we will drink his bad health."[16]
   The *Pall Mall Gazette*, however, stiffened its upper lip at
the standard of values that laughed at the deception which
victimized Billy Bolton and his father: "The idea of one college
cheating its rival of its principal player in this fashion, or of
any self-respecting collegian permitting himself to be so dealt
with, is alien to every English idea of 'playing the game.'"
There were other notes of dissent, too: the Westminster *Gazette*
found certain "amusing verbal gymnastics" in the play, but was
cool to its plotless noise and directionless energy. The *Globe*
found "too much satire and too little humanity" in the play, but
admitted that *The College Widow* "may possibly attract from
its very novelty." The *Morning Advertiser* objected that the play
"abounds in quaint exaggerations of character . . . but . . . we
regard them as freaks, or racial curiosities, rather than as actual
human beings." The *Daily News* wrote: "It is a poor thing only
made tolerable by the inexhaustible energy of the players and
the cleverness of the stage management." *The Daily Graphic*
dismissed the play as a novel but shallow oddity.
   At its jauntiest, the London reception is best represented by
the review in *The Athenaeum*:

> The American stage has sent us many productions which have
> deafened us by their din, and taken our breath away by their
> pace; but we have had nothing hitherto so full of noise and
> hurry and frenzied excitement as "The College Widow."
>   The Actors do not walk on or off the stage; they run on, they
> race off. They talk as fast again as the average English player.
> There is no underacting or dropping of the voice; ordinary

conversational passages are shouted, and shouts rise to shrieks and yells in moments of agitation.

As if this clamor and "hustle" were not sufficiently disconcerting, the author introduces a set of characters so grotesque that they appear caricatures, and these eccentrics in their banter not only use the broadest American accent, but also indulge in such a torrent of transatlantic slang that at the Adelphi glossaries are given away with the programmes. The effect of all this . . . was one at first of stupefaction.

But by sheer effort the American actors conquered their public; it laughed, applauded, and shouted in turn.

To English people Mr. Ade's university scenes must appear fantastic. If undergraduates in real life show such little respect as do those of Atwater for their President, if they are permitted to associate with town girls under no more exacting chaperonage than that of the lady who in this play asks, "Boys, have you all been kissed?" Then there is, indeed, a difference between the discipline of Oxford and that of some of the universities from which its Rhodes scholars are recruited.[17]

The College Widow infected America with a rash of plays and motion pictures about colleges and college athletics. It was the prototype of *Brown of Harvard* by Rida Johnson Young and *Strongheart* by William C. DeMille, but it has never been surpassed. Performed today, *The College Widow* would be exciting, and its satire would be accepted as both fresh and meaningful.

CHAPTER 6

Stoking the Fires

I overlooked the undying truth put into
words by Mr. Emerson to the effect that you
can't get anything in this world without pay-
ing for it, in one way or another. Every party
after eleven P.M. carries a headache. Few millionaires are happy. They acquire dollars at
the sacrifice of slumber and peace of mind.
They try to beat the game by grabbing a lot
of money and then discover that they have
brought up children who belong in the zoo.
In the heyday of my busy time as a so-called
dramatist, a lot of my good friends could not
understand why I looked and acted like a
man who had just driven home from a couple
of heart-rending funerals.

—"The Hardest $100,000 That I
Ever Earned."

WINED, DINED, and toasted wherever he went in New
York, George Ade was at the height of his popularity in
1904. Life was full and times were good. He spent his evenings
in talk and laughter; his days, in building plays, writing fables,
compiling collections, and folding money. But the seesaw began
to teeter, and Ade's sense of balance was suddenly unsure.

I *Sulu Re-visited*

Few hats hit the ceiling of Wallack's when the first-night
curtain closed on *The Sho-Gun*. Ade's fourth musical play was
a modest success; but, used to the heady champagne of thunderous applause, he was piqued at the lukewarm reception of
his new play. Opening night was on October 10, 1904, a date

that also marks the beginning of Ade's slide from the summit
of popularity. The mediocre run of *The Sho-Gun's* 125 performances was hard for him to take. "In my opinion," he wrote,
" 'The Sho-Gun' is by far the best of the musical pieces which
I have helped to build."[1]

The Sho-Gun is in a sense The Son of Sulu, for Ade tried to
recapture the oriental splendor and satiric raciness that were
successful in *The Sultan of Sulu.* In the Korean Kingdom of
Ka-Choo, Ade again pursues the American character. The program for *The Sho-Gun* states: "The 'Sho-Gun' is meant to be
an indirect treatise on the worship of titles, the formation of
trusts, the potency of the American 'pull,' the yankee commercial
invasion, legal maneuvering, advertising enterprise and other
subjects of timely interest."

The scene of this satiric folderol is laid on the imaginary island
of Ka-Choo in the Sea of Japan between Japan and Korea.
The curtain opens on a charming, oriental tableau: the ancient
ceremony of the Feast of the Ancestors at the Temple of the
Sho-Gun. The stage is resplendent with priests, monks, geisha
girls, guards, and attendants grouped around a sacrificial altar.
A choral chant sets the oriental tone, and Moozoo-May, chief
of the geisha or sing-song girls, sings a patter song with
choral responses. The effect is so obviously Gilbertian that Ade
directed: "It is desired to avoid any costume effects which will
too strongly suggest 'The Mikado.' "[2] He then proceeded to ape
Gilbert sedulously, as in the entrance of the wise and Mighty
Hanki-Pank, court astrologer and dealer in cynicisms:

HANKI-PANK

Each day I most devoutly thank
The gods for making Hanki-Pank;
   A person of such sterling worth—
   The wisest mortal of this earth.
     That I am wise
     No one denies,
   And my judgment is so faultless
   That it never can go wrong;
     And you will know
     That this is so
When I tell you that I don't intend to sing a comic song.

GIRLS

We humbly thank
you, Hanki-Pank.

Your judgment can't go wrong
And we know it when you say that you will not inflict a song.
(Act I, 9)

Hanki-Pank carries the satire until help arrives in the person
of William Henry Spangle, the confounder of Korean civilization.
Hanki-Pank has many excellent lines: "The tombstone has become the hall mark of patriotism, for the extinct politician is
always a statesman"; "Love affairs *begin* in poetry and *end* in
prose"; and "Millionaires are *never* vulgar—*eccentric* perhaps,
but *never* vulgar."

The Sho-Gun is a series of thirty-two songs occasionally interrupted by dialogue, and each song, an entity in itself, con-
tributes little to the progress of the play. From time to time
a new character colloquizes onstage to afford respite for the
audience. Tee-To, for example, intrudes upon a melodious idyl
and is questioned by Hanki-Pank about his pensiveness. He
learns that the sad young man is helplessly in love with the
Princess Hunni-Bun. Hanki-Pank's comment has a touch of
Chicago's Loop: "The Princess! Niece of the Sho-Gun! How dare
you? Isn't it strange that the ribbon-counter Lothario passes
right by the glove compartment and throws his aching heart
at the four-million dollar Myrtle whose gray-squirrel muff represents two years of his picayune salary" (Act I, 15).

Although the affections of Princess Hunni-Bun respond to
the passions of Tee-To, the commoner, their love is doomed by
custom, diligent chaperones, and Korean law. All seems lost,
when a letter for the Sho-Gun arrives. In his absence it is read
by Kee-Otori, military grandee.

Dear Sho-Gun:—

If you have in stock any second-hand ancestors or moss-grown
temples that you are ready to close out at a bargain, I am your
Huckleberry! Money talks. I am a busy man but I can spare
you an hour. Don't keep me waiting.

Yours for business
William Henry Spangle
(Act I, 27)

The insolence of the communication enrages Kee-Otori who
lusts to see Spangle's drawn and quartered carcass decorate the
city wall. The Koreans sing a prolonged song of revenge during
which William Henry Spangle ambles through the gate into

the temple of the Sho-Gun. His appearance is greeted with a
formidable silence. Spangle simply gawks at the Koreans with
curious irreverence and begins to sing "The Irrepressible Yank":

> Wherever British drum-beats sound
> Unending 'round the world,
> Wherever is some land, new-found
> Our starry flag's unfurled,
> Where'er the sun is known to shine,
> Or winds consent to blow,
> These nimble countrymen of mine
> On business errands go.
> In southern isles,
> Where nature smiles,
> They sell the ham what am—
> Upon some cliff
> Or Teneriffe,
> You'll read, "Don't be a clam."
> In England, Ireland, Scotland, Wales,
> We show our goods and make our sales.
> No other drummer can outrank
> The bold and enterprising Yank.

REFRAIN

> The Yankee-Yankee-Yankee-Yankee
> Irrepressible Yank.
> A regular traveling board of trade,
> And a two-legged sort of bank,
> If you deal with him and don't get left,
> Your lucky stars you'll thank.
> This Yankee-Yankee-Yankee-Yankee
> Irrepressible Yank.
>
> (Act I, 28)

After two more stanzas Spangle introduces himself as the
author of Spangle's Goo Goo Chewing Gum, but this fails to
impress his auditors who insist on executing the irrepressible
Yank. "I bet you four to one I don't die," retorts Spangle. "I'll
bet you *seven* to one I don't die. I'll bet you *three* to one that
you ain't alive." Spangle explains why he is in Korea:

After I made my bundle in the Goo-Goo business, I left the tall
timber and decided that I'd get in among the top-notchers, even
if I had to dig a tunnel. So, I moved over to Newport and built
a million dollar cottage. I had the kitchen finished in onyx and
used Florida water in each of the 32 bath-tubs. Every morning

I met the postman, expecting a few large pink invitations to stop over and eat with the Knickerbockers, but they didn't seem to arrive. I made inquiries, learned that in order to get in with the cold-storage coterie I needed a title and a long line of ancestors, so I started around the world hoping to pick them up (Act I, 32).

Spangle proceeds to organize Ka-Choo. He passes himself off as the walking delegate of the Executioner's Union to avoid being beheaded. Thereafter, he is a whirlwind of commercial activity. He turns Ka-Choo into a minor league Wall Street, builds pickle and "butterine" factories, promotes a national interest in Goo-Goo Chewing Gum, unionizes the workers, organizes enough cartels to place all nobles on boards of directors, forms the departed ancestors of the court circle into a trust, turns the royal palace into a department store, converts the temple of the Sho-Gun into a bowling alley, appropriates a couple of golden Buddhas as garden ornaments for his Newport home, establishes the Ka-Choo Benevolent association— "the object of which is to acquire all the property lying to the north, south, east, and west"—and considers plans for opening seven additional corporations the next day.

In the evening of his first busy day in Ka-Choo, Spangle rescues the beautiful, young widow of a Sho-Gun from sacrificial death by tiger. In fact, he has everything well under control by the time His Excellency Flai-Hai, the Sho-Gun of Ka-Choo, returns from a hunting trip. The entrance of Flai-Hai occasions a Gilbertian flourish entitled "The Sho-Gun of Ka-Choo":

FLAI-HAI AND CHORUS
As the ruler of my party I made up my royal mind

GIRLS
Made up his royal mind

MEN
Made up his royal mind

SHO-GUN
That I'd be a public idol of—the rough and ready kind.

WOMEN
The rough and ready kind

MEN
The rough and ready kind

.   .   .   .

REFRAIN

> For, I'm stren-u-ous and scrappy,
> Yet, de-lighted, bluff and happy,
>   I'm the Sho-Gun of Ka-Choo,
>   Full of most surprising capers:
>   Keep my picture in the papers—
> I'm the Sho-Gun of Ka-Choo.
>
> (Act II, 27-29)

Flai-Hai is told that Ka-Choo has been invaded by a promoter who has flaunted, broken, or raped every Ka-Chooian value. The Sho-Gun attempts the assassination of Spangle, but the walking delegate of the Executioner's Union refuses to be killed by non-union labor. The Sho-Gun is nonplused:

SHO-GUN. (In despair) Merciful Buddah! My treasury depleted, my household organized into a Union, my authority upset by these legal trickeries—*what* am I to do?

SPANGLE. In a case like this, there is only *one* thing for a *wise* ruler to do—compromise with the labor leaders, increase the taxes and make a new issue of bonds.

SHO-GUN. A *bond issue?* Who will take our bonds?

SPANGLE. *I* will—provided you give me the customary inside rate.

SHO-GUN. But I have no security to offer.

SPANGLE. Yes you have—the best in the world.

SHO-GUN. What's that?

SPANGLE. The title of Sho-Gun.

THE OTHERS. Sho-Gun!!!

SPANGLE. I came here to get a title. When an honorable businessman schemes and maneuvers to get hold of nearly all the money in the world it is not the money that he wants—he wants to see his wife's name in the pink supplement. He wants the hoipolloi to look up to him. I want to be a *Sho-Gun*. I want to walk down Broadway and have people say: "There goes the Sho-Gun of Ioway"—They won't know what it means, but they'll vibrate just the same (Act II, 35).

Flai-Hai abdicates the throne, and William Henry Spangle of Ioway becomes Sho-Gun. He weds the royal Omee-Omi and returns to his native land a social success.

The Sho-Gun, a frothy farce infinitely superior to the wilted wit of *Peggy from Paris,* is fully the equal of *The Sultan of Sulu.*

Its dialogue is crisp, its satire has thrust, and its slang is imaginative. Slight but delightful, *The Sho-Gun* amused audiences and won moderate critical applause.

Life condemned the play as a cheap imitation of *The Mikado*,[3] but the New York *World* hailed it as "One of the best comic-operas of the lighter vein. It is bristling with color, movement, mirth and melody." The *Herald* was moderately disappointed: "Not that 'The Sho-Gun' is a failure—far from it—the music is sparkling—at times—the dialogue is crisp and snappy—at times—and the laughs are hearty—at times."

The *Press* praised Hanki-Pank for "the true Ade epigrammatic sting," but it found the play not up to the quality that audiences had a right to expect from Ade's pen. "Startling originality marks neither the book, the score nor the stage settings of 'The Sho-Gun,'" said the *Telegraph*, "And yet all have escaped the commonplace. The best feature is its dash." The *Daily Tribune* saw *The Sho-Gun* as a series of musical productions interrupted by vaudeville, and the *Evening Post* was indifferent to the book and antagonistic to the score. Most of the reviews found Gustav Luders' music merely passable.

The *Evening Mail* said the play was "clean, straightforward and compact," and then added:

> If George Ade ever takes a turn at satire—ever lets the smile that lurks in the corners of his mouth start downward—ever lets a venom steal into his wit, there will be such a sizzling of hides in various upholstered places as will make old Dean Swift's spirit shake its half-Morocco sides with a recrudescent joy. Look to yourselves, my masters, to cover get you in mad haste, my complacent lords of democracy and princes of merchandise, if this young scribe should ever be seized with the notion that society needs not merely to be laughed at, but flayed.

"This piece is not characteristic of George Ade at his best," wrote *The Theatre Magazine*. "Mr. Ade misses the trick somehow. It is plain that he did not give the time to it."[4] This observation strikes the truth: George Ade did not give enough time to *The Sho-Gun*.

II *The Ace of Spades*

If Ade was vexed at the lukewarm reception given *The Sho-Gun*, he was to be appalled by the chill that greeted his next play, *The Bad Samaritan*. The new comedy limped through fifteen performances, and was an outstanding failure in every way. When it collapsed, Ade's career as a playwright was mortally stricken. He rallied with *Just Out of College* which appeared in the same season, but even this moderately well-received play survived for only sixty-one performances.

Opening at the Garden Theater on September 12, 1905, *The Bad Samaritan* was hastily written and reached Producer Savage just ten days before the first performance. "It was written for Richard Golden and it was all wrong," wrote Ade. "It had a bad title, and the people wouldn't come out to see it even the first night."[5] But Savage contributed to the play's rejection by exaggerating Ade's familiar pageantry. Director George Marion backed Ade in protesting against the travesty:

> The "Bad Samaritan" I claim went overboard at Atlantic City, washed away by a tidal wave of detail. Producer Savage, who wanted the scene of the board walk realistic, so cluttered it with a throng of ensemble that it destroyed the continuity of the plot, swamping it beyond recovery. At dress rehearsal, Ade and I were sitting in the auditorium when the procession of extras were taking possession of the scene. Ade always abhorred the comic strip rube, and as one came in sight followed by his brood, George elbowed me saying, "look at that freak with the chin whiskers, get them off." Another came in sight from the opposite side of the stage. "Marion, look at that one. Get those whiskers off" and on the appearance of a third, he jumped up and shouted "This play doesn't need an author, it wants a barber to shave the cast."[6]

The Bad Samaritan was so bad that Ade thought it not worth the bother to have it copyrighted. Enough of the mangled manuscript remains, however, to piece together the outline of the plot. Uncle Ike Gridley, summering at the New Boston Hotel in the hinterlands of the cornbelt, is the victim of his own generosity. He has bestowed his fortune upon his only nephew, Alonzo Gridley, who has a wife with social ambitions. Elizabeth Gridley doesn't mind the money, but she finds Ike, a hides-and-tallow merchant, a little hard to take. She enlists her husband's aid, and together they force the penniless old merchant into a Lear-like exile. He is put on a dole and rusticated.

In exile, Ike has one confidante: Suzanne Wheatley, housekeeper at the hotel. "Did you ever hear of a man gettin' foolish with his fountain pen?" he asks Suzanne. "I signed *one* paper, and when I got through I had what the boy shot at. It's a long story and nobody around here knows all of it—"?[7]

Suddenly, Ike is paid a flying visit by Alonzo and Elizabeth. Through a technicality, the assignment of his fortune to his nephew is void, and Isaac Gridley is returned to prosperity. The conniving pair try to hoodwink the old man into signing a new document, but he is too shrewd to be taken in. He intends, nevertheless, to be kind and understanding toward Alonzo, but he is affronted by Elizabeth. Ike is fond of Suzanne Wheatley and insists on introducing her to his kin. Suzanne puts out her hand to Elizabeth:

MRS. ALONZO: (Arising and pretending not to see the extended hand.) Alonzo, let us be going back to the station. Really, I feel as if we were on exhibition.

MISS WHEATLEY: (Embarrassed) Well, I just wanted you to know that we were glad to see you.

IKE: (Stepping in) This is Miss Wheatley, the housekeeper here at the hotel—been a very good friend of mine.

MRS. ALONZO: I dare say you mean well, but isn't this rather unusual, the formal introduction of servants?

IKE: Servants?

MISS WHEATLEY: I'm sorry. I didn't mean to—

IKE: That's all right, Miss Wheatley.

MISS WHEATLEY: (About to break down and cry, starts toward kitchen door.) I'll go in the house if I'm not wanted.

IKE: (To Mrs. Alonzo) She's no servant. She's the housekeeper. (With rising anger) As far as that's concerned the first time I saw you you was a *hired girl*. (Mrs. Alonzo shrieks)

MRS. ALONZO: Oh, how *dare* you?

ALONZO: Don't Uncle. You know how sensitive she is.

IKE: Well, some other people can be sensitive, too. (Very angry.) It's a fact ladies and gentlemen (addressing crowd): she was working at a cheap lunch counter . . .

MRS. ALONZO: Alonzo, take me away from here.

IKE: (Continuing) When Alonzo wanted to marry her I said *yes,* go ahead and marry her. She's a poor girl, only one dress to her back—

MRS. ALONZO: Oh! Oh!

IKE: (Continuing)—Ain't accustomed to luxuries—if you give her a home she'll appreciate it and be thankful. And so he married her. And now she ain't sure whether she's Mrs. Potter Palmer or Mrs. Stuyvesant Fish (56-57).

Poor and humiliated, Alonzo and his wife leave the New Boston Hotel. Ike, having regained his business and fortune, decides to reward his friends: "You've been good to me when it didn't look as if it'd pay," he tells them, "and now I'm goin' to pay you back with interest. This is my *second time on earth.* Pack your grips, everybody—we start for town this afternoon" (74).

The second act takes place in an apartment in the St. Burleigh, the most fashionable hotel in town. All goes well for a while, but soon Ike's country friends change: Eugene Spillers, who wanted to be a country veterinarian, now wants Ike to buy him a membership in the stock exchange for a paltry $78,000. "I find that if you help a man once or twice he's *grateful* in a *way*," observes Ike. "If you keep on handin' things to him, he begins to feel after awhile that he's got a right to sit in your lap and take it out of your pocket. I'm through."[8]

In Act II Suzanne Wheatley and Ike fall out. The cause of their estrangement is one of literature's great mysteries, for the manuscript is mutilated at this point. Suzanne, however, returns to New Boston; Ike takes his retinue to Nirvana-by-the-Sea. Disgusted with the greed and ridiculousness of his friends, Ike is befuddled until he barges into Alonzo and Elizabeth who have the rolling chair concession on the boardwalk. Contrite and deflated, they are happy to see Ike. Their daughter Jessie, as genuine as Suzanne Wheatley, finally wins Ike over to her parents' side.

Abandoning his parasitic entourage, Ike decides to pay his debt to New Boston with a library, but the citizens scorn the gift. Here again the manuscript is in tatters. The fragments reveal that Ike has picked up Suzanne's old homestead on a foreclosure sale, intending to turn it into a library. The ensuing complications are resolved somehow (the manuscript won't tell) and the final curtain falls on the betrothal of Ike and Suzanne.

The Bad Samaritan groans with grotesque small-town types: Bluford Higgins, cheap, cunning, covetous proprietor of the New Boston Hotel: litigious H. Calhoun Galloway, big-city promoter; Homer McGill, unsuccessful inventor; Andrew Jackson Jones, garrulous hotel clerk; Signor Pietro Gargelini, effete professor from the conservatory; Eugene Spillers, slangster; Belle Hinkle, an incipient Melba; and Mrs. Butler of the Ladies Literary League.

Much of the satire in the play hit the absurdities of the *nouveau riche,* but it was lacking in quality. Slapped together as though by a gag-writer from vaudeville, *The Bad Samaritan* was day-old bread loaded with the lower-priced spread. With few exceptions, the press condemned the play as unworthy of Ade and as not worth the attention of the discriminating playgoer.

"George Ade is quite evidently a man wholly at the mercy of his inspiration," wrote the New York *Daily Tribune.* "Until the 'Bad Samaritan' his inspiration did not desert him, but in that play he foundered. The Ade formula was there, flashes of the Ade wit illuminated it, but spontaneity and life were lacking." "The story of 'The Bad Samaritan' is nearer burlesque than comedy," wrote the *Times.* "A musical comedy without music," observed the *Sun* dryly. The *Herald* was one of the few papers which gave *The Bad Samaritan* a ringing cheer:

> "The Bad Samaritan," which was presented at the Garden Theater last night, achieved the prompt success which his "The College Widow" and "The County Chairman" had scored. The new play substantially deserved it.
>
> There was success in the air from the outset of the evening. In the first ten minutes of the play the house bubbled with merriment, which continued thenceforward to the end. If sometimes in the course of the evening there seemed lacking something of the freshness of the author's earlier work, still the three hours of the performance were filled with so many rattling good things that they gave one little time for odious comparison.

"Utterly hopeless," lamented *Everybody's Magazine.*[9] *The Theatre Magazine* observed that the play "at no time rose above the level of commonplace farce. Even the dialogue lacked the usual pungent humor we are accustomed to associate with this author. The whole suggested haste and smacked of the conventional pot-boiler. The idea on which the story is hung is interesting enough, and with happier treatment a capital comedy might have evolved from the material at hand."[10]

The Bad Samaritan was obviously a bad play, for its conception was faulty. Ade turned the devastation of laughter on the hazards of openhanded but stupid philanthropy and sought to mine humor from ingratitude. He underestimated his audience, expecting them to find comic enjoyment in a gallery of freaks that are infuriating, despicable, silly, or spineless. Even though audiences were predisposed to laugh at anything Ade offered, *The Bad Samaritan's* pot never came to a boil.

III *The Great Pickle Swindle*

Ade and Savage parted company after the failure of *The Bad Samaritan*, and Charles Frohman produced Ade's new comedy *Just Out of College* on September 27, 1905. But Ade needed more than a new producer to stop his slide at the box office. *Just Out of College* lived for only sixty-one performances in a season that introduced plays that were to run for two years. Ade's trouble was his inability to sustain wisecracks for two and a half hours. He had burned himself out. He began to re-use situations, characters, and techniques that had been successful in his former plays. But their bounce was gone.

In his new play Ade returned to the campus "cut-up" for his hero. John Worthington Swinger, fresh out of the "culture factory," seeks his fortune. He has fallen in love with Caroline Pickering, only daughter of Septimus Pickering, the pickle king. Septimus has reservations about Swinger when he lists his possessions as "three suits of clothes—one suitcase—one kodak—one banjo—one tennis racquet."[11]

Septimus' first interview with Caroline's ambitious suitor is constantly interrupted by solicitors, union delegates, and a comic office boy. Swinger, sensing the pickle king's exasperation, dazes the intruders with Latin and Greek and then propels them through the door. Septimus admires the youth's gall, and Swinger's stock makes a sharp rise when Septimus meets Professor Bliss, Mrs. Pickering's choice for Caroline. Bliss is an "apostle of repose" who admonishes the pickle king about his abrupt temper:

SEPTIMUS. (to Bliss) Did you ever hire a lot of flat-headed imbeciles and pay them good wages and then have 'em throw you down? (On this speech Bliss has arisen and gone toward him with his hand raised.)

BLISS. Mr. Pickering—sh-h-h!

SEPTIMUS. What's up?

BLISS.   Don't you recall the beautiful teaching of Mahala, the Persian?

SEPTIMUS.   Never heard of him.

BLISS.   He says—"Control thyself." Be master of thy soul. Repression—poise—relaxation—you seem to lack them.

SEPTIMUS.   Did McNally, or whatever his name was, ever try to run a shipping department? (33).

Septimus decides to give young Swinger a chance to prove himself. As a tribute to Swinger's colossal brass, Septimus offers to stake his prospective son-in-law to five thousand dollars. The money is to be invested shrewdly by Swinger, who must show a distinct profit within three months. Swinger refuses the offer, however:

EDWARD.   Mr. Pickering, really you surprise me. A man of your experience. Five thousand! The way business is conducted nowadays, a man with five thousand dollars is like—I'll tell you what he's like—a poker player with one white chip.

SEPTIMUS.   (Aghast) Wh-a-at!

EDWARD.   You know—at first—when you spoke there—I thought you were just kidding me.

SEPTIMUS.   Well—of all the colossal, monumental—(Falls into chair—swallowing)

EDWARD.   Five thousand dollars! That wouldn't last a man from here to the corner. I tell you what it would do—it would just about pay my cab-fare looking for a chance to invest it.

SEPTIMUS.   Say! Stop! I can see that I've got you sized up altogether wrong. I'll take a good, firm hold on this chair and then you let me know how much you think I ought to let you take.

EDWARD.   Well—ah—I should say—ah— about a hundred thousand.

SEPTIMUS.   Don't go away! I'll come down in a little while. Suffering Cornelius! A hundred thousand.

EDWARD.   (Coolly) You know—I don't expect to open a peanut stand or a soda fountain.

SEPTIMUS.   (Sarcastic) Going to build a railway, I suppose.

EDWARD.   Mr. Pickering, be reasonable. You know that five thousand is simply out of the question.

SEPTIMUS.   (Rises) Mr. Stringer—

EDWARD. Not Stringer—Swinger.

SEPTIMUS. Whatever it is, I'll tell you what I'll do. As a slight tribute to the most gigantic gall that I ever encountered—I'll let you take twenty thousand.

EDWARD. Well, that's a little better (44-45).

Act II is set in the midst of the Pure Food Exposition wherein Edward Worthington Swinger is busily promoting Bingo Pickles, a newly marketed product in competition with Pickering's Perfect Pickles. Actually the Bingo Corporation, headed by N. W. Jones, a female businessman who owned Swinger's college boardinghouse, had offered the Bingo product to Pickering. Pickering was not interested, and Swinger has invested his money in Bingo Pickles as a silent partner. His idea is to make a big splurge with Bingo Pickles and then sell out to the pickle trust headed (unknown to Swinger) by Septimus Pickering.

The complication is resolved through a series of revelatory muddles: Professor Bliss turns out to be the estranged husband of Miss Jones, having deserted her years before; Septimus Pickering buys Bingo Pickles for $100,000; Caroline and Swinger are united; and Mrs. Pickering receives her comeuppance through the exposure of Bliss whom she has been pushing on the Coordinated Culture Clubs as a bona fide genius.

The Ade pageants abound in *Just Out of College*. In the spectacle of the Pure Food Exhibition, the stage directions intend an all-out effort by the cast:

> All available Extra People may be thrown on for this opening picture, some sent across up stage—some down stage looking curiously at the exhibits and then passing on. Have Elderly Gentleman of eccentric appearance, to be indicated hereafter, as Collector, move from one exhibit to another, taking a sample from each and then exit.
>
> Here may be any number of Bingo girls, and they wear uniform fancy costume—pattern may be fantastic—letter "B" on apron—or a design of pickles on skirt. Suggestion of extravaganza (49).

In Act III another pageant is set in a railroad station. Eccentric travelers, newsstand vendors, ticket agents, colorful porters, a Runyanesque information clerk, and the regular characters are at liberty on the stage.

Just Out of College is a cut above *The Bad Samaritan*, but it is not in the same league with *The County Chairman* and *The*

College Widow. Repartee and "flip" dialogue flutter across the stage like confetti. Though Ade's wit sparkles brightly, it is not enough to illumine his slender plot with happy substance and satisfying humor. The characters are pasteboard. Swinger is an opportunist who proves himself superbly effective as an un-ethical businessman, thereby winning the admiration of his future father-in-law, who heads a trust that he prefers be called "a combination." Neither Swinger nor Pickering is the butt of satire; they are the heroes of the play beside whom the other characters show to disadvantage.

Swinger, it is true, does not know that Pickering heads the trust that he is "sandbagging," for a red-blooded American boy would never swindle a *friend.* In a letter to Frohman, Brander Matthews is ready to sacrifice even this shred of grace for the sake of a sounder plot:

> I want to thank you for the pleasure of seeing "Just Out of College." I always enjoy Ade's plays, as they are so racy of American character.
> But I think I see why this play has not been as well received as the "Chairman" and the "Widow." It is because Ade has not seen the strength of his own story. "Jiggsy" Swinger is a clever fellow; and the audience wants to see him make good. He ought to go into the Bingo Company, *knowing* he is bucking against Perkins [Pickering], intending to win. He ought to be shown in the second act intent on making the Bingo business a paying proposition, working seriously and ingeniously. He ought to keep his female partner up to getting a big price out of Perkins. And we, as spectators, want to *witness* the details of the sale to Perkins, the woman doing it, but Jiggsy in the background, (Visible to us) and pulling the wires. Then, we want to *see* him, in the 3rd act, go back to Perkins with the $20,000 to return, and with it at least $30,000 more of his own. This scene ought to balance the admirable scene at the end of act first; it ought to be the counterpart of that, with a turning of the tables on Perkins, when Jiggsy explains how he made the money. Thus, the young fellow would be shown as actually doing something for the sake of the girl he wants. His speech may be amusing as it is, but his purpose ought to be serious.
> Excuse my butting in to what is not my business![12]

The breeziness of Swinger and the hard-headed realism of Pickering are amusing, but their conflict is not enough to sustain the play which is a breezy, gag-girdled farce.

The newspaper reviews of *Just Out of College* are split. On the one hand the New York *Evening World* shouted: "A roaring success!" On the other the *Globe and Commercial Advertiser* scoffed at Ade's "shovelling in the sands of the commonplace." "The obvious trouble," said the *Herald,* "is that Mr. Ade has come to think that for the sake of his audience he must be perpetually funny, and as a result the spontaneity of his wit naturally halts now and again."

The *Evening Telegram* observed that the play has "one of those pleasing twists to the story that hold you long enough to entertain but not long enough to make you feel that the author is doing much more than lightly searching his own immediate and superficial experience."

"Laughs now and then were there," wrote the *Evening Sun,* "but they were more the laughs which come from a minstrel's joke than the mirth which is aroused by a good scene in a clever play. It was a joker, not a playwright who inspired them." "Disappointing," said the *Evening Mail.* The *Press* judged the comedy "one of those exasperating plays that is neither quite good enough to assure great success nor quite bad enough to indicate downright failure." "The new piece," wrote the *World,* "must be set down as a decidedly clever piece of work. Its merit lies almost wholly in its dialogues, for it is built on rather conventional lines and it makes small pretense of plot." The *Sun* said it was now clear that "Mr. Ade has not only failed to live up to his early promise but has raised the question whether he has not already given us the full measure of his capacities." The *Daily Tribune* observed that Ade got caught in the complications of his play and "as the snarl became tighter his characters and his play became more conventional till the second curtain fell on a scene of the tritest farce."

Just Out of College had a brief run on Broadway but it enjoyed a longer run on the road. New York playgoers were beginning to wonder about George Ade. Had he already sold all of his best wares? Was he going to continue hammering out cheap imitations of his earlier work? The answer came with *Artie* in 1907.

CHAPTER 7

From Bad to Vaudeville

> I had not learned that purgatory and play-
> house may be synonyms. I thought playwriting
> consisted of preparing a script and then
> cashing checks. No one had tipped off to me
> the inner secrets of the torture chamber.
>
> —"The Hardest $100,000 That I
> Ever Earned."

ADE SPENT the greater part of 1906 abroad. Upon his return to Broadway, he hacked out another failure. He was through as a popular playwright, but he didn't know it. The theater was in his blood, and no cure has ever been discovered for this affliction. Ade's major literary efforts continued in the field of playwriting until the day finally came when one of his plays could not reach Broadway.

I Patchwork Quilt

The Bad Samaritan marks the low point on Ade's dramatic chart, but *Artie*, produced October 28, 1907, keeps it close company. *The Bad Samaritan* had fifteen performances; *Artie* had twenty-two. *Artie* not only died a quick death in New York, but caused its creator the ultimate humiliation of being rejected on the road. The average Ade play toured for two or three years, but *Artie* couldn't stumble through one season.

Artie is the character who was born in "Stories of the Streets and of the Town," but *Artie* the play is not based on the newspaper sketches. The newer Artie is a more sophisticated wiseacre involved in a specific plot, and he is not merely a vehicle for Ade's slang.

Artie did not represent wholly fresh material. It was a patchwork of bits and techniques culled from Ade's previous work. The play opens at a dance with a typical Ade pageant: "This whole scene a noisy crowd effect, introducing a few good character types who pass from check room door across, shaking hands with Carroll and then off L. If they are embarrassed, ill at ease and awkward, so much the better. They need not wear good clothes, but they must have clean collars and hair combed and wear button-hole bouquets, or dance programmes hanging from lapels."[1]

Artie, who crashes the Annual Bazaar and Ball of Wood-workers' Union No. 17, spars wittily with several characters until he sees Mamie Carroll with whom he falls in love instantly. Mamie, cool but interested, grants Artie permission to call. Act II is set in front of the Carroll home on Cedar Street a week later, when Artie calls upon Mamie. Mrs. Carroll, a jealous parent, is subdued by the artful hero at their first meeting: "Mrs. Carroll, I lost my mother when I was a kid—I can *just* remember her and that's all. I've lived around bum boardin' houses all my life—no *home*, no *women folks* to keep me in line— I'm no *angel*, I know that, but if a nice, good motherly woman like you was to take a little interest in me you'd find me right there tryin' to do the square thing" (16). Artie can hurdle any obstacle either by the brilliance of his wit or by his guileless manner. He is a bit of a dandy, too: "He gets fourteen dollars a week—spends *ten dollars* for clothes—the rest he just *fools away on room and board,*" reports his friend, Miller.

Act II is a period piece full of young love and laughter, front porch tranquility, nineteenth-century character types, and "fly" talk. While engaging in his suave banter, Artie spies a surveying crew trying its best to act unobtrusive. His interest is piqued, and he shadows them. Discovering that they are surveying for a new suburban spur of the Metropolitan Elevated Railroad, Artie plots to control a half dozen houses that stand in the right of way:

> As far back as I can remember—my father and mother tryin' to keep house on *nothing* per week. That's why their little offspring is going to get his. If they don't want me to get it, they'd better lock it up. . . . On what I can save out of fourteen a week I'll have at least a thousand dollars when I'm ninety-two years old. Now these old fellows that lecture at the YMCA tell a young man to be honest and hard working and *save* a little every week. But you can gamble that ain't how they got *theirs*. Only one way in this world to get money and get it quick and that is, grab something that somebody else needs and make *him* pay *your* price for it (21).

Artie's only other justification is that "It's no crime to hold up a corporation." Consequently, he plans to hold up the Burleigh Company by taking an option on six houses. He pledges his seventy-five dollar watch to gain a week in which he must raise five hundred dollars to secure the option. Artie, who happens to be in the employ of Burleigh Company, is found out and loses his job. Fortunately, he just happens to have a wealthy uncle who puts up the cash for the option, but he refuses the additional sum Artie needs to conclude the purchase.

Burleigh, sure that he can wait out Artie's option, has been courting Jimmy Larkin, a political hack certain to be elected alderman of the district which must grant the requisite franchise to Burleigh's Metropolitan L. To insure the election of Larkin, Burleigh must "influence" the president of the Young Men's Independent Club of the Nineteenth Ward. The young politician turns out, of course, to be Artie. The resultant deal: thirty thousand dollars for Artie's real estate, an important position in the Burleigh Company, and an apology from Burleigh for clouding Artie's reputation in the eyes of his beloved and temporarily estranged Mamie.

Artie is a trashy play lumpy with stock jokes about marriage, girls, politics and politicians, real estate, and business. It is gusty with crackling slang, slapdash satire, and breezy dialogue; but spontaneity is absent. Artie is a cheap counterfeit of Edward Worthington Swinger of *Just Out of College.* He is a tricky opportunist, flashy, superficial, flippant, unwholesome, and a master of duplicity and misrepresentation. *Artie* is a kind of picaresque drama in which the rogue is a bloodless drugstore cowboy who becomes a successful cheat.

Clayton Hamilton discussed Artie's emptiness at length in *The Forum*:

> The failure of the play was inevitable. It told the story of a clever and flippant young man who jollied his way to material success. To use for a moment the language of the author, what Artie handed out was josh. Mr. Ade should have foreseen that a successful drama could not be patterned out of the deeds of such a hero. In the first place, it was impossible to awaken for him any serious sympathy from the audience, because the hero never felt any very serious emotion. The love interest of the play was weak and ineffective, because Artie made love just as flippantly as he did everything else, and his best girl seemed to exist chiefly for the sake of being jollied. Furthermore, since it was a fore-

gone conclusion that Artie, by his cleverness and wit, would get
the better of anyone who tried to thwart him, it was impossible
for the dramatist to create any feeling of suspense as to the
outcome of the action. The struggle was never serious and therefore never really moving.

The play failed merely because it was lacking in emotional
appeal. Cleverness alone will never interest an audience. The
spectators did not care for Artie as a person, because they were
never allowed to fear for him and seldom lured to love him. To
make a comedy, as has been frequently remarked, is a very
serious business, and the best of comic plays are those that
often tremble on the verge of tears.[2]

The New York press was sharply divided in its judgment
of *Artie*. The *Herald* observed that "a fable in slang is worth
two on the stage . . . those in the audience who had not read
the 'Artie' sketches began mentally to slang the fables." The
Evening Sun, however, had a higher opinion: " 'Artie' is a slight
little play, half farce, half genre, half fable in slang (we were
never good at fractions). But slight as it is and mixed as it is,
it is unfailingly amusing and wholly delightful and unmistak-
ably George Ade." The *Daily Tribune* observed: "The intention
was to depict an image of merry impudence, which yet should
be amiable and pleasing, if not winning: and that intention has
been accomplished." The *Times* wrote: "a crazy quilt full of
bright little patches. . . . Artie has most of the good lines, and
the other people generally stand around with long theatrical
spoons feeding him the laughs."

Ade consigned *Artie* to the growing limbo of his regrets,
but three box office failures in a row had him on the ropes.
Fortunately his spirits were raised somewhat by the modest
success of his next play, *Father and the Boys*. The play opened
at the Empire on March 2, 1908, and it ran for eighty-eight
performances in New York and for three years on the road.

II *The Good Fight*

Lemuel Morewood, dealer in wool, is the hero of *Father and
the Boys*. In spending his life bagging money, Lemuel, a widow-
er, has neglected to help his boys develop moral fiber. The
resultant dilemma faced by Lemuel is the basis of Ade's comedy:
father would give his business to the boys, but the boys are
busy giving the business to father.

William Rufus Morewood, the elder son, is typed by the set for his office. "A desk plainly marked 'William R. Morewood' . . . is surmounted by small silver tea-service, bouquet, several photographs in fancy frames, cigarettes in holder and any other fancy articles which may suggest a rather luxurious type of fashionable man. Above this desk on wall may be pictures which might appeal to the taste of a young man infatuated by the glamor of the exclusive set."[3]

The office trappings of Thomas Jefferson Morewood, the other son, reflect contrary but no less frivolous interests: "On top of this desk two pairs of boxing-gloves; Indian clubs and dumb-bells lying on floor beside desk. Crossed fencing foils and tennis racquets on wall, together with pictures of football teams, boat-races and any track events. Possibly two or three silver cups on shelf or on top of desk" (8).

The plainness of Lemuel's desk marks him as simple, direct, and unpretentious. He is holding things together, and the boys are humoring him by letting themselves be kept on the payroll. The tragi-comic seed of *Father and the Boys* is handled by Ade with unusual sensitivity. Tobias Ford, Lemuel's lawyer, consults his employer on the results of several years' work. Lemuel treats him with a strange and pathetic disinterest:

FORD. You're a queer man to me—sometimes.

LEMUEL. (*Looking up*) Queer? How?

FORD. We've been working for years on this consolidation. I go out West to perfect it—come in with the glorious results—(*Show-him blue-bound papers*)—right in my hand, and you begin talking about something else.

LEMUEL. (*Squaring around*) Yes—about my boy Billy and about these girls. Why? (*Suddenly adopting emphatic manner.*) Because all the consolidations and all the new money in the world don't mean anything to me—unless—(*Hesitates.*)

FORD. Unless what?

LEMUEL. Unless it means something to my boys. I may be a big gun in the business world, but I'm afraid the boys regard me as a joke.

FORD. I wouldn't say that. (*But not contradicting him very strongly.*)

LEMUEL. Waited years for this day to come—a dozen big

jobbing concerns—all tails to my kite. And now—(*Rises, manner changing.*) It's no fun to fly the kite.

FORD. (*Consolingly*) Nothing wrong with the boys?

LEMUEL. Wrong? You bet there isn't—they're my boys, and I wouldn't trade 'em for anybody else's boys—but you can see for yourself—planned it all out—college—then Europe—then in here as partners. I've made this business so big it needs three men to carry it. Result: Billy's one ambition in life is to dance all night. Tommy, I think, would like to be strong enough to throw the Terrible Turk (17-18).

Lemuel, who eventually decides to teach his boys a lesson, finds his opportunity in Bessie Brayton, who is to entertain at a soirée the boys are giving at the Morewood home. Inveigled into a roulette game, he breaks the bank to the consternation of the boys. Their astonishment is completed when he airily leaves the party with Bessie on his arm.

A wholesome, outspoken Western girl, Bessie appeals to Lemuel, who learns that she has a half share in a Nevada gold mine. Hard-pressed for cash, Bessie has decided to sell her mining stock to a disreputable gambler who has been preying on Morewood's sons. Lemuel sees an excellent opportunity to help Bessie, destroy the despicable Major Didsworth, and liberate his boys. He leaves for Nevada with Bessie, and the boys organize to give pursuit. In a swift-paced series of comic vignettes, the play ends in the West: Major Didsworth is exposed as a rascal; the gold mine pays off; Bessie is re-united with her true love; the boys are reclaimed in character; and Lemuel Morewood finds peace of mind.

Ade had wrestled hard with his tendency to dramatic effervescence, and he succeeded somewhat in controlling his unruly talent. There is more plot in *Father and the Boys* than in any other Ade play. This is not to say that Ade was completely successful in making a carefully plotted play, but he succeeded to the extent that the critics were aware that he had tried—and failed. His effort, moreover, cost him the ebullient sparkle which had always been his most lustrous quality. There were few hearty laughs in *Father and the Boys,* for the lines of the play were witty but uninspired. William H. Crane and his supporting players must have added the touch of life that can make a play that wheezes in the closet breathe freely before the footlights.

Ade's characters in *Father and the Boys* were unoriginal. The play is cluttered with stock types, obvious relationships, trite situations, and tired witticisms. It has moments of freshness, but they cannot redeem the comedy from the list of potboilers written by Ade since *The College Widow*. Ade was a fading playwright. He saw the curtain beginning to fall, and he made a strong effort to halt its descent. He spurned the pageant, fought the element of vaudeville in his work, and tightened up the joints of his plot; but he probably suspected that his string of failures was to be increased by one more, for he left for Bermuda on the day *Father and the Boys* opened at the Empire.

In general the press was favorable, indeed many of the reviews were laudatory: the New York *Morning Telegram* found *Father and the Boys* and *The College Widow* tied for greatness in the Ade canon. "A clever, crisp and clean cut comedy," wrote the *World*. "A capital comedy," said the *Herald*. "Chockful of chuckles," chortled the *Evening Sun*. "Clean, honest and boisterously amusing," said the *Globe and Commercial Advertiser*. "It is clean in sentiment, frequently sparkling in dialogue and contains enough of its author's genial satire to keep the audience in ripples of mirth," wrote the *Evening Mail*. "Fairly bubbles and burns with mirth, color and action," said the *Press*. "One of the welcome events of the season," wrote the *Tribune*. "By far the best play George Ade has written since 'The College Widow,'" said the *Evening World*. "Fun without intermission," said the *Evening Telegram*. "There isn't a line in it that would make a Skaneateles dominie blush." Although the *Sun* charged that *Father and the Boys* sank rapidly into farce, it found the play "brisk and enjoyable . . . told with the utmost spirit, with racy, picturesque dialogue. . . . It is farce that often trembles on the verge of comedy."

Many of the newspapers remarked upon the part which Actor William H. Crane played in making the play a success. "There is not the slightest doubt that the star lifts the piece with a powerful jerk over the footlights till it strikes you right between the eyes," observed the New York *Evening Mail*. "This was a case of play and actor being indispensable one to the other," wrote Metcalfe of *Life*.[4]

The modest success of *Father and the Boys* was immensely pleasing to Ade, but he was still troubled about his future in the theater. There were still a few plays in him, but the old zest was gone.

III *Love at the "Brain Hatchery"*

The Fair Co-Ed was written for the Harlequin Club of Purdue, but Charles Dillingham talked Ade into its production on Broadway. The play, Ade's first musical comedy since *The Sho-Gun* in 1904, opened on February 1, 1909, for a run of 136 performances.

The Fair Co-Ed, a musical adaptation of *The College Widow*, omits the football game. The plot is simple: Cynthia Bright is the only co-ed remaining at Bingham College (Bingham was Atwater's rival in *The College Widow*). The faculty has decided to end co-education and to promote scholarship, but lovely Cynthia owns the heart of the student body. And, in addition, she also controls the affections of Professor Josephus Cadwallader, a big gun on the campus. Cynthia's love, however, belongs to Davy Dickerson, who is under an academic cloud: Professor Cadwallader insists that Dickerson's graduation depends upon his making up all of his "freshman work in trigonometry, osteopathy and domestic science . . . sophomore work in physchology [*sic*], entomology and veterinary science . . . junior work in horticulture, agriculture and menticulture, to say nothing of . . . senior work in all . . . courses."[5] Davy must also make up one hundred and eighty hours of drill in military science. Somewhat discouraged, he contemplates leaving Bingham for the world. But life is not so simple. It is discovered that Cynthia's father had left a deathbed request that she marry a Bingham graduate. Davy must now forsake the world and remain at Bingham. But Cynthia is worth it.

The play promises to be amusing by the end of the first act, but hope dissolves in the shenanigans at Bingham's annual military ball in Act II. For some unfathomable reason, ostensibly because Davy is submerged in make-up work, Cynthia decides to attend the ball disguised as an Annapolis midshipman. She captivates all the girls, and their escorts group to torpedo the charming middie. Faithful Davy discovers their plot just in time to save her from disgrace and public humiliation.

The last act of *The Fair Co-Ed* is a hodgepodge of silliness. Each of the graduating seniors declares his love for Cynthia and is wittily rebuffed. Davy Dickerson's disloyalty in effecting the escape of the doomed midshipman results in a court-martial at which Cynthia appears to recite, verbatim, Portia's speech on the qualities of mercy. Davy beats the rap. In the meantime he has taken a prodigious number of examinations and re-examinations in order to qualify for both graduation and Cynthia. He has managed to pass all but astronomy, and he is at the point of despair when Professor Cadwallader finds him. One of the questions which Davy had failed to answer was withdrawn by the examining committee. Another was substituted. If Davy can answer this question, he gets his degree.

"Here is the question," says Professor Cadwallader: "What is the name of the star of the first magnitude discovered by Professor Richter of Leipsic University August 1, 1885?" (30). Pad and pencil in hand, Davy stands in helpless ignorance gazing stupidly at Cynthia who is wringing her hands in agony. Finally the worthy professor takes the pad from Davy's hand and discovers to his elation that Davy has named the star correctly not once but twenty times. The answer: Cynthia. What else? True love blossoms. Curtain.

Many of the characters in *The Fair Co-Ed* equate with types found in *The College Widow*: Cadwallader is President Witherspoon; Davy Dickerson is Billy Bolton; Bob Chester is the stupid athlete, Silent Murphy; Squab Dingle is Bub Hicks; Ernest Grubb is the pedant, Copernicus Talbot; and Grouch Hubbard is blood-brother to Matty McGowan.

The satire on college professors has the same sharp nip too:

REED. (*To Cadwallader*) Member of the faculty?

CADWALLADER. (*Looking at Reed severely*) Why should you doubt it?

REED. I don't doubt it. You look a little bit hungry—you're not as well dressed as the students—your hat is a sight (16).

In summary, *The Fair Co-Ed* never makes good on the sprightly promise of the first act. The humor is watered; the plot collapses in the second act; the dialogue is often silly; the incidents are uninspired; the lyrics are banal and sticky; the pageants are colorless echoes from *The College Widow*; the characters lack blood; and even Ade's genius for observation is curiously limited.

Gustav Luders' music, a snappy cast, and several medleys of college songs undoubtedly pepped up *The Fair Co-Ed* and sustained it for one hundred and thirty-six performances; but, though it landed on the profit side of Dillingham's ledger, it did nothing for Ade's reputation. The play was designed as a gift to Purdue; as such, it was handsome. On Broadway it was no gift at all.

The press received *The Fair Co-Ed* with divided opinion. The New York *Evening Mail* wrote: " 'The Fair Co-Ed' is kid stuff. . . . The plot will not strain anybody's brain. . . . Mr. Ade has not overburdened his libretto with side-splitting lines." The *Herald* said, on the other hand: "Mr. Luders music was as bright and sparkling as any one could ask, and altogether 'The Fair Co-Ed' proved all that its authorship entitled the audience to expect—and that means a whole lot." "The whole play had a healthy, snappy atmosphere, and the audience liked the old-time college songs," wrote the *Times*. "Sprightly," commented the *Daily Tribune*. The *American* said "there was no end of enthusiasm at the Knickerbocker Theater last night," and implied that the star, Elsie Janis, was largely responsible for the success of *The Fair Co-Ed.*

The *Sun* critic pointed out an innovation: "There isn't a regular opening chorus. Not a chorus girl appears in the whole first act . . . but a large number of 'chorus men' made good for almost the first time in the history of musical comedy." Channing Pollock of *The Smart Set* wrote: "Such pleasure as one derives from the performance comes from the youth and exuberance of the young people employed in telling the story. The entertainment, as a whole, is attractive only in spots, notably when the chorus is singing a medley of old college airs or exhibiting the ingenious 'business' of a good football number. Mr. Ade's wit seems to have been dragged into the play by its boots."6

Because *The Fair Co-Ed* was profitable, Dillingham asked Ade for another musical play. "From the very start of my dealings with the managers," wrote George Ade, "I wanted to get away from the musical plays, but these same managers have stars under contract, and musical plays, which look so trivial and easy-to-write, are hard to get. The first thing I knew, Mr. Dillingham had me talked into fixing up a play for Fred Stone and David Montgomery."7 *The Fair Co-Ed* went on the road with Elsie Janis, and the royalties were still pouring in when *The Old Town* opened at the Globe Theater.

IV *Bagpipes and Balancing Poles*

George Ade's last Broadway play was a musical extravaganza, *The Old Town,* which opened on January 10, 1910. He was less than proud of the entertainment and failed to have it copyrighted. The manuscript has been lost, but an impression of the play can be raked from its reviews.

The play is built around two scapegraces who steal the clothing of two personages about to arrive in town. The thieves enter upon a debauch of zany impersonations that require various disguises: Scotch, Japanese, Swedish, and English among others. Dozens of vaudeville specialties enliven the stage. Reported the New York *Evening Mail*:

> Few comedians are called upon to walk a slack wire fifteen feet above the level of the stage, as Mr. Stone does in the first act, or could accomplish the feat without the aid of a net as wonderfully as he did yesterday.
>
> Even the fact that he had a balancing pole need not detract from the credit due him. Later on he scaled a garden wall with a rope and was suspended in mid-air by merely twisting it around his leg while he helped along a comedy scene; and toward 11 o'clock he swung a lariat in such wonderful circles that some one called him the Ternazzini of the hemp. Throughout the evening, furthermore, Mr. Stone indulges in such limber calisthenics and contortions that the audience laughed its collective head off.

In addition there were a bagpipe specialty, an English pony ballet, novelty dances, and a band of singing suffragettes. "The story? As the boy said when asked for the apple core, 'There isn't any'—just two hours of fun and frolic, fast and furious," wrote the *Herald*.

The reviews of *The Old Town* were both kind and objective. "It is nothing more than a gay song-and-dance show, with the nimble Fred Stone ever in the lead," wrote the *World*. "The typical George Ade lines are missing and the plot is so diaphanous that the footlights devour it," said the *Evening Mail*. The *Times* wrote:

> Summing it all up, as far as anybody can sum up a show of this sort in a hurried account, it may be said that the specialties, the girls, and first and foremost, Montgomery and Stone, of course, will give it such popularity as it is to have. Neither Mr. George Ade nor Mr. Gustav Luders would go down to posterity as public benefactors if they had to depend on "The Old Town" for fame.
>
> The book is neither better nor worse than many others that come through the general process of slicing and peeling required for the introduction of songs and specialties, but one does rather expect a scintillating line from George Ade now and then.

Observed George Jean Nathan, for *The Smart Set*: "'The Old Town' . . . written by George Ade . . . caused even some of the latter's best friends to withdraw their names from his own famous I-Knew-Him-When Club. Mr. Ade must have slipped on the Banana Peel of humor when he committed the book of the play. It was left to Stone's megavoltic dancing to win the entire approbation of hands that itched to clap, but for the most part, had to be content with scratching."[8]

The Old Town ran for one hundred and seventy-one performances before its demise. Ade's career as a Broadway playwright was buried with *The Old Town,* but he didn't recognize his condition. He made a musical adaptation of *Artie* for the Harlequin Club of Purdue, and he wrote *U.S. Minister Bedloe,* a comedy which drew breath in Chicago and died in Boston before its projected New York appearance. As far as Broadway was concerned, *The Old Town* was George Ade's dramatic swan song.

V *Instant Musical*

Ade's last musical play, *The City Chap,* was apparently designed for the entertainment of Purdue and the residents of Lafayette. The play ran for three performances (March 28-30, 1910) at the Dreyfus Theater under the sponsorship of the Harlequin Club of Purdue. Whether or not Ade hoped to bring *The City Chap* to Broadway is not known. The play is a warmed-over hash of scraps from Ade's former plays. It is derived principally from *Artie,* but characters are lifted from *Just Out of College, The County Chairman,* and *Father and the Boys.*

The City Chap differs little from *Artie* in its plot. As Jack Hamilton, the new Artie, says to Annie Belle, the counterpart of Mamie: "All I've got in the world is a hundred thousand dollars worth of *property* that I haven't paid for. I'm sitting behind a *pair of deuces,* with *one white bean* in front of me, trying to bluff a millionaire."[9]

The opening pageant is set on Annie Belle's street with a "couple of men of the subdued Lonesomehurst variety . . . pushing baby perambulators," delivery boys, girls with wildflowers, and a constable leading an "automobilist" by the collar. This scene blends into the opening chorus:

> A little side street in the country,
> A burg on the edge of town,

A little side street in the country
Where faces are smiling and brown.
Where every one's happy and glad they're alive,
With never a sorrow or frown.
There's nothing can beat or even compete
    With a country town.

(Act I, 9)

Sassafras Livingston cakewalks into *The City Chap* as Tansy Lippincott: "Two things hard for a colored man to do," says Tansy. "One is to *get* money—another is to *keep* it. . . . Money in the bank is like *silk underwear*—you know it's *there*—you kind o' enjoy *havin'* it there but, doggone it—you ain't makin' no impression with it" (Act II, 16).

Ade's wit flashes like heat lightning throughout *The City Chap,* but as a musical comedy it is a poor thing: the situations lack proper motivation and its effects are hazy. The play is a clumsy collage of characters from former plays and of miscellaneous vaudeville numbers haphazardly glued together with slang.

VI *A Career Ended*

Aside from writing a few one-act plays, Ade abandoned the theater after the failure of his last full-length comedy, *U.S. Minister Bedloe.* This comedy opened at Chicago's Blackstone Theater on December 31, 1910. After a three-week run, it went to the Park Theater in Boston on January 30, 1911. The play lacked the vitality to reach Broadway.

U.S. Minister Bedloe recounts the adventures of Colonel Jackson Bedloe, American newspaper publisher and would-be diplomat. "After a man gets his *money*—that's when he begins to sigh for *glory*," says the colonel. "I feel that *I'm entitled* to a good long rest. You know, in *this* country when a man wants a *good rest* he applies for a *government job*."[10] The colonel (he was once on the governor's staff) asks for a diplomatic post in the Argentine; but, as his secretary pointed out: "Another fellow wanted that—and the other fellow used to go to college with somebody *else.* . . . *Yale* and *Harvard* stuff! If you can't give the *yell* you don't get the *barrel of flour*" (Act II, 2, 2a). The colonel is finally tossed a post in remote Caribay, a microscopic nation in South America.

The Bedloes find Caribay oppressively hot and intolerably

dull. The oleaginous prime minister of Caribay, Senor Miguel Cabrera, has designs on Kate Bedloe, the colonel's beautiful daughter. For a month Kate has not heard from her sweetheart, Bob Deane, and she is beginning to show a perverse interest in Cabrera. Actually Bob is on his way to Caribay leading a group of insurrectionists who purpose the destruction of Caribay's tyrannical government. The mess of events that follow involve: the Cabrera-Kate-Bob triangle, the antics of the insurgents, the colonel's apparent policy of neutrality, and the necessity of keeping Mrs. Bedloe in the dark about all matters that might disturb her. These situations are the substance of *U.S. Minister Bedloe*. Everyone is eventually captured by everyone else. The colonel's Yankee shrewdness leads ultimately to the victory of the insurgents; to the liberation of Bob Deane, who is to be executed; to the rescue of Senor Cabrera from a mob; and to the preservation of the colonel's specious policy of neutrality. Though the cannons roar and the walls of the embassy come tumbling down about her, Mrs. Bedloe's nervous condition is not troubled; for the ingenious colonel convinces her that she is experiencing the height of Caribay's fiesta season.

The usual pageant occurs: Act II opens on the veranda of the International Club at San Quito, capital of Caribay. Long drinks, white suits, native costumes, Spanish music, and a busload of dark-skinned character types romp upon the stage.

The play is larded with slang by Edwin M. Chester, secretary of the legation and former sports editor of Bedloe's newspaper. Chester's principal lament is that he is two thousand miles from the nearest rathskeller. His explanation of why Bedloe accepted the Caribay post is in the patter of the fables: "He was about to pass it up—but a couple of *fluff* Senators that he had toasted in the *paper* said they were going to *corral* his *Angora*" (Act I, 5).

U.S. Minister Bedloe starts well in its Springfield, U.S.A., setting; for Ade is on firm ground with the testimonial ceremonies of Springfield's Commercial Association, Thursday Club, and other bands of patriots. But when he moved his characters to the alien palms of the tropics, his play came apart; and audiences witnessed the painful spectacle of wit and satire searching for a foothold in a zany plot. Too much of the action occurs offstage, and the interminable satire on the Monroe Doctrine, South American instability, politics, the Department of State, and foreign diplomats slows the action to a prosy walk.

The characters in the comedy are cut from the old patterns: Bob Deane, the college fraternity boy, who gives revolution the old college try; Colonel Bedloe, the shrewd, homespun American of the county chairman type; Edwin Chester, the "fly" Artie-like slangster; Katherine Bedloe and Gertie Hooper, sweet young bloodless things with lines; the Honorable Cecil Thornby, British minister to Caribay, the quintessence of the Empire; and Herr Otto von Maxhausen, German minister to Caribay, a sausage-and-beer Prussian of the stock and stupid type.

Something was lacking, too, in the quality of Ade's wit in *U.S. Minister Bedloe*. Gone was the slam that his lines once had. It took him pages to reach an effect that he staged in a dozen lines in *The College Widow* and *The County Chairman*. Ade had lost the touch.

Ade's last comedy was, therefore, the longest and most tedious of his plays. There is little wonder that it died in Boston; it is surprising that it lived to make the trip from Chicago. "I knew it was a goner ten minutes after the curtain went up," Ade told his biographer. "But I had to stay there [Chicago's Blackstone Theater] all evening while the blood slowly froze in my veins."[11]

The reviews of *U.S. Minister Bedloe* in the Chicago papers were unenthusiastic. The *Tribune* wrote: " 'U.S. Minister Bedloe' appeared to us to be a bit trite and slow and unagitating. It moved last evening, to us at least, in a somnolent dog trot, despite some acute and satiric observation by the author and much eager, if not always accurate acting by the star." The *Examiner* wrote: "The plot, the characters, the situations, the very scenery begs for song and dance. A very amusing farce might have been a convulsing musical comedy." The *Journal* concurred. Ade's old friend Amy Leslie of the *Daily News* wrote the most generous review and called Ade "a perfect master of sharp keen dialogue." The Boston press was cool to the play. The *Evening Transcript* reported it "a little thin." The *Globe* saw it as "a dramatic trifle of the flimsiest construction imaginable."

Luther B. Anthony of *The Dramatist* wrote the most scathing review: "If George Ade's past dramatic work has been conspicuous for one thing more than another it is the absence of tangible Plot. In 'U.S. Minister Bedloe' he is seized with the sudden desire to incorporate this disregarded ingredient. The result is a hodgepodge of conventional theatric contortions serving mainly to obscure the author's native wit."[12]

Ade's last full-length play sank quickly and deservedly into oblivion, and George Ade bid a sad farewell to the American stage.

VII *Excuses*

Although the highest returns of his money-making career came from his years as a dramatist, Ade decided that "the pains and penalties and trials and torments and disillusionments involved in writing for the stage were an offset to the Captain Kidd revenues."[13]

Ade's failure to sustain his popularity as a playwright smarted with a persistence that lasted for years. If he had continued to click at the box office, he would have continued writing plays. In later years he wrote: "One reason why I do not wish to write for the stage is that while I was turning out plays the whole illusion of the theater was destroyed for me. When I went to a play I saw nothing except a lot of wheels going around."[14] His inability to slough off adverse criticism is a reason less inept:

> If a man writes a book that does not arouse public interest the book dies a quiet death on an under-shelf, and if the author discontinues the clipping service he need suffer no actual pain except that caused by a private and well-concealed disappointment. But if he writes a play that fails to score he is pilloried in public. He is scalped to slow music on a high pedestal with an amber light turned on the scene of his humiliation and thousands of people apparently enjoying the fun.
>
> Viewed from almost any direction, the first night is the best imitation of purgatory that I have encountered. Even when the final ring-down leaves the playhouse tingling with the electrical knowledge of a sure success, the playwright feels so much like a wet towel that he can not find any joy in the situation. If I could remain away from rehearsals and eliminate the first night I would rather work at writing plays than do almost anything else.
>
> So long as I am compelled to attend rehearsals and then participate in the agonies of the first night I would rather do almost anything else that was not too criminal.[15]

After the failure of *U.S. Minister Bedloe* in 1911, Ade wrote a few one-act plays and flirted with Hollywood;[16] but he was no longer a working playwright. He shifted his astonishing productivity to other projects.

CHAPTER 8

Curtain Raisers

"No one else has known how to interpret
America to itself in certain phases with such
unfailing security of touch to such satisfying
effect, and we must not think this effect is
cheap and common because the material it
works is so. A masterpiece is a masterpiece,
and mastery resides in the quality of the
doing, and not the material of it."

—William Dean Howells

ADE MIGHT HAVE WRITTEN more than a handful of
skits and one-act plays if it had paid. His talent for drama-
tizing one idea in a single act was of a high order, but the
profit was low. His first venture in this form, *The Back-Stair
Investigation,* was produced in Chicago in 1897. It was a satire
on the corrupt but colorful shenanigans of Chicago politics,
but, when the skit was staged, Ade was mortified at having
"committed either a misdemeanor or a crime."[1] The manuscript
of *The Back-Stair Investigation* has been lost.

In 1898 Amy Leslie, a Chicago drama critic, gave a supper
party for May Irwin, the comedienne. She told Miss Irwin about
a vaudeville sketch, *Mrs. Peckham's Carouse,* that her co-worker,
George Ade, was toying with. Miss Irwin begged Ade for the
playlet. Remembering *The Back-Stair Investigation,* Ade de-
murred; but the actress offered him two hundred dollars to
write the skit and promised to assume all risk. In a few days
she had the manuscript. Years later, Ade wrote:

> She [May Irwin] put the little play into her trunk and kept
> it a couple of years before trying it out. Every time I met her
> I began to apologize for taking money and giving her something
> which she could not use. I couldn't hand the money back to her

because I didn't have it, but I felt very guilty and remorseful. Finally it happened that up in Boston she was doing a farce called "Mrs. Black is Back," written by George Hobart. The players kept speeding it up until they had the running time cut down so that the comedy would not fill out the evening, even after they held back the overture and strung out the intermissions. May Irwin dug my play out of her trunk and used it as a curtain raiser and it must have got over pretty well because after the first performance she put the little play at the end of the bill after the regular comedy was over.

That was well over twenty-five years ago. May Irwin has played it ever since when she needed a one-act "vehicle." Flo Irwin played it all over Europe. Just this year May Irwin has been doing it again over the Orpheum circuit. On the moderate royalty basis of fifty dollars a week, the amount which an author receives for any kind of a good vaudeville skit, the royalties to date would have been about $10,000. That is why I have stopped apologizing to May. It must be remembered that when she purchased the play she was the only person in the world who suspected that I was a dramatist and her check for $200 looked like all the money in the world.[2]

May Irwin's skit, *Mrs. Peckham's Carouse,* is the story of Horace Peckham, a thirsty lawyer, and his wife, Susan Peckham, leader of the Daughters of Total Abstinence. Mrs. Peckham blunders into her husband's office and sees a visitor, Mr. Barrett, with a bottle of whiskey. Peckham has gone for a water chaser and in the interim his guest is besieged. The angel of Total Abstinence, in a rage of righteousness, calls Barrett's wife from the reception room and tells her that Barrett is drunk. Peckham returns but is warned into a closet by Barrett. After a spirited harangue, Mrs. Peckham bustles back into the office for a pair of gloves that she had forgotten. She sees the drinks and renews her harangue. Peckham is still in the closet. Mrs. Barrett enters upon the scene, sees her husband with two drinks and a woman:

MRS. BARRETT: Aha! I've caught you at last, have I?

BARRETT: (Approaching) Look here, Fanny, let me tell you . . .

MRS. BARRETT: No, Thomas Barrett, you have deceived me for the last time. (Sees bottle and glasses) And *drinking too! Both of you!*

MRS. PECKHAM: What does this mean, Mrs. Barrett?

MRS. BARRETT: You'll find out what it means, Mrs. Peckham, when I get you into court. I've been watching you two. I know about the letters you've written. (Both are surprised) *Now* I find you here in this private room, locked in and *drinking* together.

MRS. PECKHAM: (Aghast) Drinking! Drinking!

BARRETT: Nonsense! Fanny!

MRS. BARRETT: Don't deny it! Why, I received a telephone message saying you were *drunk*.

MRS. PECKHAM: Yes, but *I—I* sent it!

MRS. BARRETT: You! Aha! I might have known. . . . You wanted to make trouble between me and my husband, did you? Well, Mrs. Peckham, it will come out at the trial!

MRS. PECKHAM: *Trial? What trial?*

MRS. BARRETT: *What* trial? The *divorce* trial. I'll expose you— you BRAZEN CREATURE! You've robbed me of my husband—my— oh, Tom, why did you do it? (Falls into a chair . . . and weeps violently; at the same time Mrs. Peckham is swaying about with her hand on her breast)

MRS. PECKHAM: (Weakly) Divorce trial, caught in this room— with him, drinking—Oh—Oh—horrible—Oh—Oh—! (Collapses into a chair . . . in a fainting condition.) [3]

Barrett pours both glasses of whiskey into Mrs. Peckham to revive her. When she comes out of her fainting spell, the office boy, Henry, enters the room with a cork-screw. He is made the goat and is sent on a two-week, paid vacation on the pretense of being fired. Mrs. Peckham insists that the men smash the bottle of liquor.

MRS. PECKHAM: (Triumphantly as crash is heard) There! We have done our duty!

PECKHAM: Yes, thank heavens, Susan! *You* got the only two drinks that ever came out of that bottle.

MRS. PECKHAM: And the strangest thing is, Horace, that they didn't affect me at all.

(Mrs. Peckham, complacent but sleepy. Mrs. Barrett laughing at men who walk upstage cursing their luck in pantomine)

HENRY: (Coming into the room) Mrs. Peckham the Daughters of Total Abstinence are waiting for you to address them.

MRS. PECKHAM: Well, you tell them that I said to adjourn the meeting. Something very pleasant has happened to me, and I can't come.

This delightful skit, combining gentle satire, economy of situation, swift, sparkling dialogue, and deft characterization, delighted audiences whenever it was played. "Mr. Ade has adorned the dialogue with his usual fresh and racy humor," wrote Clayton Hamilton, "and contrives to create a great deal of fun in the brief compass of an act."[4] *The Theatre Magazine* thought the play "delicately humorous" and filled with "inoffensive foolery."[5]

So popular was *Mrs. Peckham's Carouse,* and so identified had it become with May Irwin, that she guarded her rights jealously. May Irwin's sister Flo Irwin, played Mrs. Peckham, but had to pay May fifty dollars a week royalty and was "only permitted to play Chicago and west of that city."[6]

I *The Musical Janitor*

Another early skit by Ade is *Il Janitoro,* a burlesque of grand opera, originally set to music and played at the Lamb's Club in New York. Later, with success but without permission it was presented at the Empire Theater in London.

The spoof reveals itself best by quotation:

MRS. TAYLOR: I think I smell smoke.

MR. TAYLOR: She thinks she smells smoke.

MRS. TAYLOR: I think I smell smoke.

MR. TAYLOR: Oh. What is it? She says she thinks she smells smoke.

MRS. TAYLOR: What does it mean, what does it mean?
This smell of smoke may indicate,
That we'll be burned—oh-h-h, awful fate!

MR. TAYLOR: Behold the smell grows stronger yet,
The house is burning, I'd regret
To perish in the curling flames;
Oh, horror! horror!! horror!!!

MR. AND MRS. TAYLOR: Oh, sad is our lot, sad is our lot,
To perish in the flames so hot,
To curl and writhe and fry and sizz,
Oh, what a dreadful thing it is
To think of such a thing!

And on, and on. Finally the janitor knocks politely on their door to inform them that the house is burning:

JANITOR: Such news I have to tell.

MR. TAYLOR: Ah, I might have known
             He has such news to tell.
             Speak and break the awful suspense.

JANITOR: I come to inform you that you must quickly fly.
             The fearful blaze is spreading,
             To tarry is to die.
             The floors underneath you
             Are completely burned away.
             They cannot save the building,
             So now escape I pray.

MRS. TAYLOR: Oh, awful message,
             How it chills my heart.

Etc., etc.—"But why go further," breaks in Ade. "The supposition is that they continued the dilatory tactics of grand opera and perished in the flames."[7]

II *Political Squeeze Play*

The Boss of the Ward, copyrighted October 13, 1899, satirizes the genteel businessman who would dabble in politics without soiling his honor. William Ashton, a young lawyer, is running for alderman of his ward. To gain the nomination he must straddle a shaky fence between tavern-owner Jimmy Dinkel, the boss of the ward, and Mr. Skinner, president of the reform league and arch foe of Dinkel. Ashton manages the support of both men, but the effort is destroying his marriage. Mrs. Ashton, suffering virtual widowhood, decides to set up a squeeze play with her husband as the sponge. She invites Dinkel and Skinner to call, but she doesn't tell Ashton.

Dinkel arrives first, and Mrs. Ashton insists that her husband serve liquor to their guest. While Ashton explores the basement for a bottle of whiskey, Skinner calls to say he will be a few minutes late.

D.———Say, let me talk to him (Goes over and takes receiver away from her. She makes pretense of resisting.)

Mrs. A.———Oh Mr. Dinkel I'm afraid—

D.————Now, that's all right, lady. I've been wanting to get
a crack at this fellow (into phone) Say, you! How's that? Yes,
Mr. Ashton's down in the cellar openin' a few bottles of booze
but if there is anything you've got to say, you can say it to me.
I'm his campaign manager, understand. (Pause) How's that?
Will he close the pool rooms? I should say not. (Pause) Come
again. Oh, you do, do you! You want to raise the license to fifteen
hundred a year, is that all? That's a good thing. Say we'll just
fool you guys. I'll tell you just what I think of you. I think you
are a billy-goat. (Ashton enters at right with tray and bottles)
What's that? Do I represent Mr. Ashton. Well you bet I do. And
say just listen to this—If he's elected this ward is going to run
wide open. Oho! Is that so? Well, say, you do come over here an'
I'll take you out and set you on top of a lamp post. (During this
talk into the phone A. has been standing at right of stage holding
tray and walking [*sic*] at D. puzzled. Mrs. A. is between them,
listening and concealing her amusement.)

A.————Dinkel! Who are you talking to?

D.———— (Hanging up phone and turning around) How's that?

A.————I say who were you talking to?

D.————I was just shooting it into that little reform stiff—
the one with the skilligans on his face.

Mrs. A.————Mr. Skinner.

A.————Skinner! (He may either drop tray and bottles on
floor or else stagger and then slam tray on table, upsetting all
of the bottles. Then he rushes over toward D.) Look here! What
in thunder do you mean by using such language as that to a
friend of mine and over my telephone too.[8]

Mrs. Ashton's triumph is complete as her husband orders
Dinkel out of the house. Ashton's political ambitions are ashes,
and the play might well have ended on this comparatively high
note. Ade, however, has Dinkel run into Skinner on the porch:

(Noise of conflict outside. Mrs. A. and A. retreat to rear of stage.
Presently D. enters dragging super made up a small man with
white wig and side whiskers, clothes torn, collar loose, etc. pulls
him down stage and drops him in a sitting posture. Skinner
looking around dazed.)

D.————There's your friend, Mr. Skinner. (Quick curtain)

Substitute finish————

D. runs in disarranged, pursued by Skinner who carries a big revolver. D. runs once around the stage and then throws up his hands and tries to hide behind Mrs. A. A. pushes Skinner away. Skinner flourishing revolver trying to get at D (19).

The Boss of the Ward makes its point that politics is a dirty, bare-knuckles business that will have no truck with either the squeamish or the ethical. The playlet is a pedestrian farce lacking the charm of *Mrs. Peckham's Carouse*.

III *"Just Fun"*

In 1904 Ade produced *Bird Center: Cap Fry's Birthday Party,* an episode in the social life of Bird Center, the locale of a popular cartoon series by John T. McCutcheon. The piece was written for Anna Morgan, noted Chicagoan and devotee of the arts, whose salon was the headquarters of The Little Room, a club boasting a distinguished membership: H. B. Fuller, Hamlin Garland, Melville Stone, George Barr McCutcheon, Ade, and many Chicagoans of social preeminence. *Cap Fry's Birthday Party,* a dramatic festival with a part for everyone, contained thirty-four characters plus bits for "Villagers, Visitors in Town, Policemen who are never around, etc."[9]

Nothing happens in this elastic skit. Each character simply steps up, congratulates Cap on his birthday, and speaks a little piece. There is Cap Fry himself, a wild soldier and a tame husband; J. Milton Brown, the model of Bird Center aristocracy; Smiley Greene, the friendly undertaker who presents Cap with a floral piece on which is written "at rest"; Wilbur Fry, noted musician who has written a comic opera about the Dearborn Massacre; Mrs. Roscoe Fry, the commandant; Mrs. Riley Withersby, the social lioness; Miss Myrtle Peters who dotes on society; the Mysterious Stranger, and dozens of others. The one unifying element in this arch pageant is Cap's collection of pickle dishes: every guest presents him with a pickle dish:

WALPOLE: Captain Fry, as President of the Bird Center Society for the Prevention of Race Suicide, I wish to present you with this magnificent emblem (removing tissue paper) an imitation cut-glass pickle jar. Remember what the poet says:

You may break, you may shatter
    The vase if you will
But the scent of the pickles
    Will cling round it still (6).

Enlivened by male quartettes, female solos, and miscellaneous recitations, *Cap Fry's Birthday Party* was an evening of "just fun."

IV *Poverty and Pride*

Marse Covington (1906) is the story of Captain Covington B. Halliday, a remnant of the old Southern aristocracy. Proud and poverty-stricken to the point of hunger, he seeks admittance to a fashionable gambling club. Looked upon as a pest by the club owner, he is turned away; but an old darky, once a slave of the Hallidays and now an employee of the club, takes pity on the old man:

HALLIDAY.   Where is the person who conducts this establishment? He shall answer to *me!* I come here not to *soil* my hands with the sordid tools of his nefarious trade, but to meet a friend— with whom I am interested in certain large enterprises. I am turned away—told that the place is closed. As I start to go—an acquaintance comes from the house—informs me that the place is *not* closed! Why has this insult been put upon me—*why?* (*More loudly.*)

DAN.   Hsh-h-h! Please Marse Covington—not so loud!

HALLIDAY.   Not so *loud!* Why *not?* How dare you correct my manner of speech? Are you getting to be one of these *damned Northern Negroes?*

DAN.   No, Marse Covington. I never *could* fall as low as *that.* I work in a clubhouse, but—

HALLIDAY.   Clubhouse—bah! This fellow is a *clod*, a vulgarian! He waved me airily away from his vile resort—I, a *Halliday*—I—[10]

Dan offers his former master a five-dollar gold piece which he claimed to have stolen from him years ago. Marse Covington sees through the ruse, but he permits Dan to press the money upon him:

HALLIDAY.   I have on hand several large projects of a gold-mining character. Should my expectations be realized, I hope to have an establishment of my own here in New York.

DAN.   Yes, suh.

HALLIDAY.   Nothing showy. I leave the gilt and the purple to the parvenus—a quiet, comfortable home-place like Essex Court House.

DAN.   No othah place *could* be like that!

HALLIDAY. When I am settled here I hope to take you away from this wretched place and make you my body-servant.

DAN. Yes, suh.

HALLIDAY. There will be *other* servants.

DAN. Yes, suh.

HALLIDAY. This is no place for one who has worn the livery of a Halliday.

DAN. No, suh.

HALLIDAY. I'll bid you good-night, Daniel. (DAN *is opening the door.*) If you wish to see me about that position, I'll be standing in front of the Astor House any pleasant day. (DAN *opens the door.*)

DAN. Yes, suh.

HALLIDAY. Good-night.

DAN. (*Closing the door.*) Good-night, suh. (*Door closed— business with chains.* DAN *stands leaning against it. May try first curtain here. He looks out.*) He's goin' to get somethin' to eat. Oh, *Marse Covington, Marse Covington!*

BANTREE. (*Enters and stands near doorway.*) Didn't I see Halliday in here just now?

DAN. He got in mos' befo' I knew it.

BANTREE. Well?

DAN. I threw him *out.*

BANTREE. Good! (*Exits.*)

DAN. (*Sinking down, sobbing.*) *Yes, suh, I threw him out!*

CURTAIN (276-77)

Marse Covington has a poetic singularity that lifts it well above its hackneyed theme. Ade was clearly capable of treating an emotional scene with dignity and sensitivity. Unfortunately *Marse Covington* was his only attempt at serious drama.

V *Back to the Pickle Factory*

Speaking to Father (1913) is a condensed version of *Just Out of College* (1905). The characters are old friends: Septimus Pickering, the pickle king; Luella Pickering, cultured wife; Edward Worthington Swinger, just out of college; Caroline

Pickering, sweet young thing; and Professor Bliss, apostle of repose. The abbreviated version of the 1905 play has only one change in plot. Swinger gets his investment funds from Pickering, but, instead of setting up a rival pickle business, he buys $100,000 worth of Pickering stock from Caroline, who had just received it as a gift. This rather ridiculous incident climaxes the play. *Speaking to Father* suffers from compression; for the situation, only mildly diverting in *Just Out of College,* is breathless and forced in a single act.

VI *Lady on the Make*

One of Ade's most popular one-act comedies, *The Mayor and the Manicure* (1912) was considered by its author as the best of his short plays. It recounts the adventures of Otis Milford, mayor of Springfield, with Genevieve Le Clair, a manicurist with both eyes on the main chance. The Mayor is a candidate for governor; Genevieve seeks cash. She has been friendly with the Mayor's son, a recent graduate of Atwater College, who is about to be married. Genevieve is certain that the candidate for governor wants to avoid embarrassment at all cost. She confronts him in his office:

GENEVIEVE. I met your son—he pursued me.

MILFORD. Pursued you? Great Scott!

GENEVIEVE. He bought me presents.

MILFORD. Hold on! *I* bought the presents—*he* merely delivered them.

GENEVIEVE. He made love to me—I thought he intended to marry me.

MILFORD. Marry you—You're old enough to be—

GENEVIEVE. (*Bristling up*) I beg your pardon—I didn't come here to be insulted.

MILFORD. Why did you come here?

GENEVIEVE. To demand justice—or—

MILFORD. Damages.

GENEVIEVE. (*Haughtily*) Yes, sir—damages.

MILFORD. Now we're gettin' down to business. (*Looks at watch.*)

GENEVIEVE. I followed your son.

MILFORD. Yes—you followed him so fast you got here ahead of him.

GENEVIEVE. (*Taking letters from purse*) I have the letters he wrote me—

MILFORD. (*In dismay*) Letters—did that young pinhead—

GENEVIEVE. You'll enjoy hearing them—when they're read at the trial.

MILFORD. Trial?

GENEVIEVE. For breach of promise.

MILFORD. Now, hold on just a second! Let me see if I understand this case. College boy with too much money to spend—meets blond manicure—out in the buzz-wagon—down where the near-beer flows—I'm afraid to go home in the dark. Wise manicure learns that papa has money—decides to get some of it. Am I right?[11]

The Mayor, of course, is right. After sparring with Genevieve, he plays a hunch. On his desk is a dummy telephone used to ring out tedious guests. It operates from a button on the side of the desk, and it is on this instrument that the Mayor calls Atwater's chief of police:

MILFORD. (*Into the phone*) Hello—Atwater? Chief of Police? This is Mayor Milford of Springfield. A woman calling herself Genevieve Le Clair, claiming to be a manicure, is down here trying to hold me up. Who is she? (*Pause.*)

GENEVIEVE. (*Very nervous*) You have no right to insinuate—

MILFORD. (*Into phone*) Yes, she's a blonde—(*Pause as though listening*) Oh, bleached, is she?

GENEVIEVE. (*Indignantly*) A lie—it's natural!

MILFORD. (*Into phone*) What is her real name? (*Pause*) You don't say so! (*Bus. of alarm by* GENEVIEVE) Has she ever been mixed up with any college boys? (*Pause*) Get out! Dozens of 'em, eh?

GENEVIEVE. (*Emotional bus.*) I merely met them.

MILFORD. (*Listening intently at phone, and then loudly and distinctly*) Where is her husband? (GENEVIEVE *shrieks and sinks back, half fainting*—MILFORD *hangs up receiver and hurries over to her alarmed.*) Madam, don't faint here. (*Letters have fallen to floor. He picks them up, looks at them hesitatingly for a moment and puts them back in her lap and begins patting her* hand.) Here! Genevieve! Come to! (*Slapping her hand. She half-recovers and looks up at him, terrified* [43].)

The Mayor bags his quarry, but he is troubled about the morality of his victory after reading the letters. He makes his son apologize for his insincerity and then gives Genevieve a one thousand dollar gift. Genevieve learns of the Mayor's bluff, but accepts her defeat graciously:

GENEVIEVE. (*Insinuating*) Won't you come out and have lunch with me?

MILFORD. You trot along, Genevieve. You've got yours. I had mine thirty years ago (46).

The Mayor and the Manicure is both the best and the most readable of Ade's one-act plays. The dialogue has a racy snap, and the characterization, obviously borrowed from *Father and the Boys,* is hearty and believable.

VII   *Pianos Are a Girl's Best Friend*

Nettie (1914) is a blithe contretemps about a scheming wench who never appears on stage. Billy Donelson, a young mining engineer from the West, has come east to pay court to Nettie Valentine. While he awaits her at a reserved table in an expensive restaurant, he is accosted by man-about-town Freddie Nichols, who has intercepted a note that Donelson had sent to Nettie. He tells Donelson that Nettie is not going to meet him. Donelson is furious; Nichols is circumspect:

NICHOLS. Under the circumstances, possibly you are entitled to know why I take such unusual liberties with Nettie's correspondence. . . . In the first place, I-I have known Miss Valentine about two years. I met her under rather unusual circumstances. I was walking down Fifth Avenue one pleasant morning. She was ahead of me. I passed her several times. You see, when *I* would stop to look in a shop window, *she* would get ahead of me again. She carried a small music roll. (DONELSON *sits up, staring.*) She happened to drop it. I picked it up—hurried and overtook her, she was very thankful and, strangely enough, she thought she recognized me as an old acquaintance named—ah!—named—

DONELSON. (*Who has been listening very intently, resting his chin on his hand and looking straight ahead, now interrupts suddenly*) Clark!

NICHOLS.   That's it! She must have told you. It was very *amusing*.

DONELSON.   Yes, it amuses *me*, all right. Did you ask if you might *call?*

NICHOLS.   As I remember, she wouldn't listen to any such suggestion. In fact, she wouldn't come out to dinner at first—only luncheon.

DONELSON.   She told you of her ambitions—the social prominence of her family at Altoona—the encouragement given to her by her teachers, and all that? . . . Will you pardon me one other question? You never ventured—that is, you never dared to offer this young woman any *financial* assistance? How about it?

NICHOLS.   After I had know her about six months I felt that I had a *right* to give her a *piano*.

DONELSON.   Is she making a *collection* of pianos?

NICHOLS.   What do you *mean?*

DONELSON.   I mean did she *take* it?

NICHOLS.   She *did*—under *protest*. She was most *grateful*.

DONELSON.   *Steinway?*

NICHOLS.   Certainly.

DONELSON.   Can you *beat that?* . . . Say, did you buy a *sable coat* for her?

NICHOLS.   (*flaring up*) It's a lie!

DONELSON.   (*squaring around to him*) What's *that?*

NICHOLS.   I—I beg your pardon, but I did *not!* I merely *loaned* her the money. She insisted upon giving a note—She even compelled me to put in a provision for interest, although I was adverse to accepting it.

DONELSON.   Six per cent?

NICHOLS.   I believe it was *six per cent*. Ridiculous, wasn't it?

DONELSON.   (*with sarcasm*) Yes, but it shows the right spirit.[12]

Just as their conversation ends, Jimmy Bates, collegian, appears on the scene bubbling with joy. He tells Nichols and Donelson that he is having dinner with a delight called Nettie who is awaiting him in the lounge. Bates shows them a diamond horseshoe which Nettie has always admired and will get from

him that evening. He wonders what they are doing at the table he had reserved for Nettie. He has brought a bouquet of violets along and lays it on the table. Curiously, each of the two men at the table also has violets in front of him. Bates excuses himself to get Nettie. Nichols and Donelson look at each other, take small jewelry boxes from their pockets and place *their* diamond horseshoes beneath their bouquets:

DONELSON.   It will be *such* a surprise to her.

NICHOLS.   (*taking* DONELSON *by the arm*) We must dine *somewhere.*

DONELSON.   There's only one place to go this evening.

NICHOLS.   Where?

DONELSON.   The Follies (25).

Nettie is the fastest moving of Ade's one-acters. Its conception is ingenious, and the suspense of the impending but permanently delayed entrance of the heroine is an exquisite touch.

VIII   *Aunt Fanny Takes a Beau*

Published posthumously in 1949, *Aunt Fanny from Chautauqua* was probably written shortly after *Nettie;* but, measured against the tightly knit plot structure of *Nettie, Aunt Fanny* is a plotless episode, a dramatized fable; but the dialogue is crisp and sparkling. Flossie Sherlock, Aunt Fanny's shallow-minded niece, is overcome with social aspirations. She has just inveigled Beverly Lattimore, stupid and wealthy playboy, into a tepid flirtation when she is advised that her Aunt Fanny from Chautauqua has come for a visit. Aunt Fanny is waiting in the foyer:

FLOSSIE.   (Grabbing him [Lattimore] by the arm and swinging him around, calling his attention to picture on wall which must be placed to show plainly.) Look at that—That is what is coming.

LATTIMORE.   You mean that little girl?

FLOSSIE.   Little girl! That picture was painted the year of the Centennial at Philadelphia.

LATTIMORE.   Who is she?

FLOSSIE.   Aunt Fanny.

LATTIMORE.   Aunt Fanny?

FLOSSIE.   Father's only sister—lives at Chautauqua—

LATTIMORE.   Chautauqua!

FLOSSIE.   Doesn't that tell the whole story? Think of anyone living at Chautauqua!

LATTIMORE.   Why this agitation? What's wrong with her?

FLOSSIE.   Listen! When she was eight years old she could recite one thousand verses of Scripture.

LATTIMORE.   Great Heavens!

FLOSSIE.   At ten she began making her own dresses.

LATTIMORE.   (looking at picture) I believe it—after looking at the picture.

FLOSSIE.   All my life she's been held up to me as a model—Aunt Fanny this—Aunt Fanny that—Oh-h-h! I can just imagine her—a thin old maid of forty—carries a bird cage—drinks catnip tea—looks under the bed every night.

LATTIMORE.   You mean—you've never seen her.

FLOSSIE.   The first time I was at school—the second time I ran away—this time there's no escape.[13]

Flossie and Lattimore remove all evidence of fast living: spirits and cigarettes are hidden, Lattimore is sent into an anteroom, and Flossie steels herself against the ordeal. Then Aunt Fanny breezes on stage and takes over. There is a strong hint of the chorus girl about Fanny. Flossie suggests that Aunt Fanny might like to lie down:

FLOSSIE.   You must be tired after your journey—it's nine o'clock.

FANNY.   Nine o'clock is the mere fringe of the night. I've got a lot of sleep in the bank—If there's a bed in my room, you might as well move it out.

FLOSSIE.   Father is at the club.

FANNY.   (preparing to make herself at home . . .) I'll wait till he comes back—then I want him to take me to some place with a million electric lights, a Hungarian orchestra and a bunch of blondes!

FLOSSIE.   (horrified) Blondes!

FANNY.   I've got a lot of Chautauqua to get out of my system—I'll tell you that. (Begins to sniff and move around.) Say, I smell a man (17-18).

Flossie unveils Lattimore. When Fanny learns that he is eligible, forty, and a millionaire, she vamps him. Her composure crushed, Flossie collapses on the piano stool as Fanny makes off with her beau.

IX *Immorality Plays*

Ade wrote two short plays especially for amateur players. Both were published in national magazines, rights were waived, and each play had a detailed introduction and commentary.

The first of these, *The Persecuted Wife*, parodied old-time melodrama and modern morality in a dual burlesque. This unusual exercise in travesty required the following introduction:

> In the preceding two acts it has come out that Alice, maiden name Marston, was lured from a country village by a handsome and well-dressed reptile named Mortimer Granby. Mortimer told her that their marriage would have to be kept secret for a while, because of his aristocratic connections, but in due time he would claim her "before the world."
>
> Alice has lived in retirement for years, waiting for Mortimer to keep his word, and in the meantime little Ethel has hopped into the plot to complicate matters. Now it comes out that Mortimer tricked her by a false wedding ceremony and has stolen the forged marriage certificate. Dirty work all around, but no dirtier than was usual and necessary in a good melodrama.

Following this brief synopsis Mortimer tells his victim that he intends to pay off his gambling debts by marrying a rich widow:

ALICE. Mortimer! Would you cast me off?

MORTIMER. Fool! Don't you see that I must save myself?

ALICE. I am your lawful wedded wife.

MORTIMER. (*gloatingly*) Lawful wedded wife! The ceremony was performed by Reverend John Burton, alias Blinky the Mop, alias Night-Hawk Harry—a friend of mine. (ALICE *screams.*) He knew too much (*significant pause*) and now he is sleeping peacefully in a graveyard.

ALICE. (*with feeling*) Wretch!

MORTIMER. (*in a smooth, ingratiating, but exultant manner*) So you see, my dear, I hold the trump card! I shall marry Edith, and you—

ETHEL.   Oh, papa, how can you be so cruel to my dear mama?

MORTIMER.   Bah!

ALICE.   (*falling on her knees before Mortimer, who turns partly away from her. Child goes to table and weeps with head buried in arms*) Mortimer! Acknowledge me before the world and I will forgive the past. See—I am kneeling before you. Pity, oh, pity! Remember your promises! Think of the old days. I care not for myself, but have mercy—have mercy on my child—my darling, innocent child—Mortimer! (*He starts to go.*) No, you shall not go! Mortimer!

MORTIMER.   Bah! (*Fiercely.*) Curse you! Farewell! I shall no longer bandy words. I care not if you and your accursed spawn starve in the streets. Farewell, my Alice! Ha! Ha! Ha!

After this episode, Ade commented on the changed circumstances of 1925: "The trick marriage is no longer plausible. It is introduced into the play upon the assumption that, previous to the wedding, the groom makes all of the arrangements. In recent years he has exercised no authority. He is less important than the caterer and only two degrees above the colored man who megaphones for the motors." He then re-enacts the tearful scene in terms of the mores of 1925:

MORTIMER.   Alice, I suppose you know—

ALICE.   I know everything. I know all about you bein' mixed up with this Fortescue gal—getting ready to marry her.

MORTIMER.   (*under his breath—frightened*) Damn it all—I say—

ALICE.   And me, your lawful wedded sweetie, here in this dump . . .

MORTIMER.   (*a little more boldly*) But you have no proof of our marriage.

ETHEL.   You tell him, mother. I'm fed up on this bird.

ALICE.   (*smiling at him in contempt and shaking her head—lights another cigarette*) Probably the champion pinhead of the world! I don't need proof. All I've got to do is go into court and cry.

ETHEL.   What's more, we've got a chance to sell the whole story to a morning paper for five hundred bucks. (*Quotes, marking with finger to indicate bold headlines.*) "Prominent society man deserts wife and child." And right below—a picture of the jolly old mater when she was an innocent village maiden.

.   .   .   .

ALICE. We'll suppose a case. A handsome dog puts over a phoney wedding at a road house—moving picture stuff. Later on he swipes the marriage certificate and beats it, leaving his wife and kid flat. He thinks he's sage because she can't go to a lawyer and flash any papers. But, suppose she gets out the old gat—hunts him up—and bumps him off?

MORTIMER. (*horrified*) Alice! You threaten me?

ETHEL. (*coming closer and joining, fresh and assertive*) She means that you will be lying in a horizontal position, getting colder all the time.

ALICE. And then—on every front page—"Deceived, Deserted, Betrayed—Facing the Cruel World—Trying to Support Her Baby." I know I'd be acquitted and if I ever caught you on Long Island I wouldn't even be arrested.[14]

Ade's last one-act play, *The Willing Performer*, needles the faint of heart. Cousin Gus from St. Paul visits his relatives in the hinterland. His cousin Eustace, a fair hand with a mandolin, offers to show him around. Eustace and Fred, his constant chum who plays the ukelele, introduce Gus to sweet Myrtle, the ideal girl. Gus, holding Eustace and Fred in contempt, decides to show them how it's done:

GUS: You boys have been hanging around her for a couple of years, haven't you?

FRED: About that.

GUS (to Eustace): Do you always travel as a Team? When One of you comes to see Myrtle, does the Other come along?

EUSTACE (replying): Yes, always.

GUS (to the two of them): And you bring your Implements with you?

FRED: Always.

GUS (amused): And when Both of you come to call on this Queen of the Human Race and bring those so-called Musical Instruments with you, what do you do?

FRED: We play to her.

GUS (shaking his head as if in sorrow but smiling all the time): This poor girl has not only been Neglected but she's been Tortured also. Have you ever had a definite theory as to what might happen to Myrtle when she met a real Live One?[15]

Gus is the "real Live One." He forces Fred and Eustace to play sentimental music behind a screen while he makes love to Myrtle, who responds. The pain suffered by the musical lovers is exquisite. In the end Gus has made a clinging vine of the untouchable Myrtle, and the music makers smash their instruments in comic rage.

The play, an apt dramatization of a fable in slang, has moments of high comedy and is eminently readable. Gus is Artie come back for another role, but then Artie was not so much a creature as a type—the city-bred American whom Ade found so useful and of whom he was genuinely fond.

CHAPTER 9

Frost on the Fireball

"Delighted to find such a sane and solid
outlook in any writer, the low-brows heaped
superlatives of praise upon him. But he
doesn't quite come up to his popular reputation. He was too temporary, too slight. His
fame was in part a club with which to beat
the high brows and it may owe something to
the facility with which his name fitted into
crossword puzzles."

—Bergen Evans

—"His portrayal of life is almost
absolute in its perfection."

—William Dean Howells

DOROTHY RUSSO'S *A Bibliography of George Ade* lists
about 2,500 entries, garnering virtually all the published
results of Ade's prolific pen. At least sixty per cent of these list-
ings appear in collections, for Ade was a superb businessman,
and as soon as he had enough periodical material to make
a book, he got out a pair of covers, stitched the articles between
them, and sent them to market.

I Tourists and Tombs

In 1906 Ade collected a volume of travel sketches entitled
In Pastures New. Based on his experiences in London, Paris,
Naples, and Cairo, the book satirizes the American tourist
abroad. Mr. Peasley of Iowa is the foil, but the European does
not go unscored. Peasley is derived from Brown of Mark Twain's
The Innocents Abroad, and his zany antics and outrageous commentaries enliven the book. Wearied by the "cemetery circuit,"

Peasley declares: "I can take a hundred pounds of dynamite and a gang of dagoes and go anywhere along the Hudson and blow out a tomb in a week's time that will beat anything we've seen in Egypt. Then I'll hire a boy with a markin' brush to draw some one-legged men and some tall women with their heads turned the wrong way, and I'll charge six dollars to go in, and make my fortune."[1]

Peasley has strong opinions about everything he sees abroad, and the reader is regaled with his notebook comments on London, English drama, Paris, opera hats, Marseilles, and Naples. His last letter home glows with the richness of his experience with the culture of the Old World:

My Dear Giff:—

I have gone as far up the Nile as my time and the letter of credit will permit. At 8 g.m. to-morrow I turn my face toward the only country on earth where a man can get a steak that hasn't got goo poured all over it. Meet me at the station with a pie. Tell mother I am coming home to eat.

Do I like Egypt? Yes—because now I will be satisfied with Iowa. Only I'm afraid that when I go back and see 160 acres of corn in one field I won't believe it. Egypt is a wonderful country, but very small for its age. It is about as wide as the court house square, but it seems to me at least 10,000 miles long, as we have been two weeks getting up to the First Cataract. Most of the natives are farmers. The hard-working tenant gets one-tenth of the crop every year and if he looks up to see the steamboats go by he is docked. All Egyptians who are not farmers are robbers. The farmers live on the river. All other natives live on the tourists.

I have seen so many tombs and crypts and family vaults that I am ashamed to look an undertaker in the face. For three weeks I have tried to let on to pretend to make a bluff at being deeply interested in these open graves. Other people gushed about them and I was afraid that if I didn't trail along and show some senti-mental interest they might suspect that I was from Iowa and was shy on soulfulness. I'll say this much, however—I'm mighty glad I've seen them, because now I'll never have to look at them again.

Egypt is something like the old settler—you'd like to roast him and call him down, but you hate to jump on anything so venerable and weak. Egypt had gone through forty changes of administration and was on the down-grade before Iowa was staked out.

The principal products of this country are insects, dust, guides, and fake curios. I got my share of each. I am glad I came, and

I may want to return some day, but not until I have worked the sand out of my ears and taken in two or three county fairs. I have been walking down the main aisle with my hat in my hand so long that now I am ready for something lively.

Americans are popular in Egypt, during business hours. Have not been showered with social attentions, but I am always comforted by the thought that the exclusive foreign set cannot say anything about me that I haven't already said about it. Of course, we could retaliate in proper fashion if we could lure the foreigners out to Iowa, but that seems out of the question. They think Iowa is in South America.

I shall mail this letter and then chase it all the way home.

Give my love to everybody, whether I know them or not.

Yours, Peasley

P.S.—Open some preserves (307-9).

In Pastures New is a delightfully irreverent travel book in the tradition of Mark Twain. Largely slangless, it is a readable and humorous satire on travelers, travel, and the inconveniences that attend sopping up culture at the wellsprings, shrines, and tourist traps of the Old World.

II   *A Penitential Effort*

Ade wrote one novel in his career, *The Slim Princess* (1907), a "cathartic burlesque"[2] of the painfully popular Graustarkian tale. Ade was partially responsible for the blight of Graustarkian, Ruritanian literature, for he had encouraged George Barr McCutcheon to publish *Graustark* (1901), which re-awakened a mass thirst for court intrigue, mythical principalities, and the inevitable contrast between clean-cut, red-blooded American youth and the thin-blooded cunning of effete royalty. The genre was originally touched off by Anthony Hope's *The Prisoner of Zenda* (1894). Ade's *The Slim Princess* was a penitential effort.

The Governor-General of Morovenia, Count Selim Malagaski, has two daughters, one fat, one thin: "To be more explicit, one was gloriously fat and the other was distressingly thin."[3] In Morovenia obesity is the most highly prized feminine attribute, and Kalora, the slim princess, caused profound anguish to her family. Kalora was the elder of Count Malagaski's two daughters, and Morovenian law forbade a younger daughter from preceding the elder to the altar.

Kalora's sister, waddling Jeneka, the most prized melon in the kingdom, must pine in misery, therefore, until some fool-hardy male abandons himself to the bony embraces of a mere 118-pound princess. Unfortunately for Jeneka, there was not a discoverable fool in all of Morovenia. This crisis in the internal affairs of Morovenia is resolved, in spite of several irritating obstacles, by young Alexander H. Pike, multi-millionaire American hero from Bessemer, Pennsylvania, whose principal non-financial attributes are pluck, athletic prowess, and an ability to use the gin fizz as a diplomatic weapon.

The novel bears the marks of haste, but it is effectual none-theless, having won for itself the honor of becoming a firm footnote in the history of the American novel. Ade's spare style and nimble wit skewered its game neatly, and no one who read *The Slim Princess* could ever again take unreserved joy in the ilk of Graustark.

III *Essays and Reminiscences*

By the time he was through with Broadway, Ade was a wealthy man. His brother had invested most of his savings in the rich farmland of Indiana, and its value had appreciated rapidly until he was offered almost $1,000,000 for his holdings. No longer was there a monetary spur to Ade's productivity, and, though he continued to syndicate his fables and to follow his drifting fancy into the lucrative market of the slick magazines, he made only one sustained literary effort after 1910: *The Old-Time Saloon* (1931).

At a loss to bring his talents to focus on anything of personal interest, Ade began taking orders for work. The *Cosmopolitan* got him to do a new series of fables to be illustrated by Mc-Cutcheon; a newpaper syndicate got him to revise some of his older fables and update the slang; The *Cosmopolitan* suggested *The Old-Time Saloon;* Hollywood bid high for several motion picture scenarios.[4] He filled the orders.

Ade spent the remainder of his active years churning out dozens of articles, features, reminiscences, and glib commentaries on American life. The books he published were collections of fables, magazine articles, and ephemera. The best of these vol-umes, *Single Blessedness and Other Observations* (1922), a miscellany of humorous pieces ranging from "Babies" to "Broad-way," contains the best of Ade's essays. The style, largely free of slang, still boasts the racy phrase-making of the fables: "Running a close second to Broadway in the folklore of the corn belt is that starchy strip of territory known as Fifth Avenue." "Every rhinestone that wants to pass for a diamond instinctively moves toward Broadway." In "Indiana" Ade writes: "We have grown some ivy, but we have not yet taken on moss."[5]

This book contains essays that appeared initially in the *Cosmopolitan, Century, Life, Saturday Evening Post,* and the *American.* A few additional subjects are "College Students," "Looking Back from Fifty," "Vacations," "Oratory," "Musical Comedy," "Golf," and "Christmas in London."

Ade's essays were charming, frequently nostalgic, and always warm with gentle humor. This genial brightness infused most of his later work, and there are few more entertaining and informative studies of the bygone palace of the swinging door than *The Old-Time Saloon,* which was "to many a weak mortal . . . an oasis of good cheer in a desert of sordid business activities."[6] The book is built upon exhaustive, first-hand research enlivened with nostalgia, charm, hard-headed reality, and quick flashes of revelation: "When we collect our memories of the old-time saloon we see a flushed person, somewhat overweight from flabbishness, the hat cocked over one eye, the breath spicy, the manner effusive, the morals uncertain and the wardrobe not distinguished by quiet elegance. We may get together once in a while and talk about the dear departed and his antics and laugh over the many social errors he committed and the trouble he kicked up, but who in the dickens wants to reincarnate him and turn him loose again" (173-74)?

The Old-Time Saloon appeared in the *Cosmopolitan* toward the end of Prohibition and was widely read. Ade appeared not to lament the passing of the saloons, but he was an anti-prohibitionist, and his rollicking chapters on barkeepers, barroom talk, songs and stories, the art of bouncing, favorite drinks, and the free lunch must have made many an old-time tippler howl with grief.

IV *The Literary Rotarian*

The bibliography of George Ade is glutted with ephemeral publications now difficult to find and little worth the trouble. Ade was as generous as he was businesslike, enlisting his talent in causes, dissipating his energies on flimsy projects, and playing the part of a literary Rotarian.

He wrote a pamphlet for the Olds Motor Works, "The Rolling Peanut"; he also worked on publicity copy for the American Merchant Marine Library Association, the Society for Preservation of American Ideals and Form of Government of Indiana, The National Security League, and several other organizations. He wrote the Sigma Chi creed and enjoyed promoting both his fraternity and Purdue University. He worked with David Ross to make the Ross-Ade Stadium a reality, directed war publicity for the Indiana Council of Defense, wrote news-bulletins to Purdue students in the service and edited the Purdue *Alumnus*. The list of his activities exhausts one in the reading alone, but Ade took genuine satisfaction in giving freely of his time. "Promoting things brings one into pleasant association with cheerful people," he said.[7]

Ade's autobiography, curiously the only series of magazine articles that he did not collect, reveals the man only by indirection. The image that Ade chose to project was that of a man who surrounded himself with luxury, reveled in mirth, enjoyed popularity, insisted on being amiable, and was, occasionally, perhaps, touched by loneliness. He reveals no great loves or tragedies or passions or convictions or aspirations. On the contrary, the autobiography is a clever mélange of anecdote, quip, reminiscence, commentary, and superficial confession.

Published in thirty magazine articles, the first of which appeared in the *Cosmopolitan* and the remainder in *Hearst's International Magazine*, the series portrays a man taken from behind by an overwhelming success in which he took a child-like delight. While the autobiography is an eminently helpful source for understanding Ade and the group of writers who flourished in Chicago at the beginning of the twentieth century, it is marred by Ade's obsession with cataloguing the names of his extensive acquaintance. This autobiography is the core of Kelly's biography, and it still stands as the most important block of primary material available on Ade and his backgrounds.

George Ade was a good, simple man with a magnificent gift that he packaged for the market place. It is idle to speculate on what might have become of his rare talent had it been burnished at Princeton rather than at Purdue—or had he aspired to the *Atlantic Monthly* rather than to the Chicago *Record*. Ade was unequal to the discipline and the intellectual direction needed to make him other than he was. But what he was, was quite enough. He was a skilled journalist, gifted with a talent that he turned to cash; and, if he grew rich upon the merriment of America, it was deserved, for America has always insisted upon enriching the talent that sprinkles laughter across the land.

Ade was not interested in literature or realism or high artistic purpose. He was not a crusading social critic; and, though he satirized many aspects of American society, he left social criticism, *per se*, to Mr. Dooley. Ade was primarily interested in the individual, whom he saw as being directly responsible for his own victories or defeats. The ills, problems, and aberrations of society were, therefore, not among his literary motivations. He preferred to observe and write about the personal problems and idiosyncracies of foolish, pathetic, bumbling mankind. To Ade, life was an opalescent bubble of laughter to be loved for its lightness and brightness, but seldom to be taken seriously.

He was a country boy who had hit the jackpot and found himself a popular hero. He lived like a baron at "Hazelden," his country estate at Brook, Indiana. He had a lovely home, a golf course, a legion of friends in high and low places, and the disposition and wherewithal to throw frequent picnics for hundreds of guests. He was welcome and honored throughout the land until the Depression came, eclipsed laughter, and erased the fame of George Ade within his own lifetime. When he died in 1944, America was surprised that he had lived so long.

Although few historians recognize Ade's contributions to American culture, they were significant and pervasive. He had salted the language with freshness and flushed from it the remnants of Victorian starch; he had wrung the neck of the horseplay and loosed upon the American theater a phalanx of character types that marches still; he stripped the city of its gaudy front so that the farm could see; and he made the city smell the dung and feel the calluses of the farm. Moreover, he made America laugh at itself as it has rarely laughed since; and he did so with a genius and a geniality that made those wounded by his satire delight in their wounds and beg for more.

George Ade did not set out to do these things; they just happened. He was a journalistic fireball that burned hotly for two decades before the frost of time chilled his vogue, leaving him rich and idle, and, in the end, virtually forgotten. He spent his last years reading magazines and newspapers, listening to the radio, wintering in Florida, and enjoying the homage of the dwindling coterie of devotees who cherished his work.

Few studies of American literature or culture have taken more than a passing notice of Ade's achievement. More often than not he is ignored altogether, for the tendency is to condemn Ade for his weaknesses and to yawn at his strengths. Most critics mention Ade with an airy wave of the hand and mutter some vagueness about the fables and their crippling slang, but that Ade made substantial contributions to American drama has gone largely unrecognized. While it is true that Ade was incapable of mastering dramaturgy, it is equally true that he wrote wholesome, humorous, simple American plays that influenced the American theater in spite of their obvious faults.

The public responded to entertainment that was clean, fresh, and free of the slapstick and the dialect idiocy that passed for comedy in the first decade of this century. Ade brought vulgarity and clownish stupidity to heel; sparked the enthusiasm of the American playgoer; and, before the boot wore thin and the buskin frayed, succeeded in making theatrical history. He plunged a drain deep into the swamp that sucked light comedy into the mire of Weber and Field's Music Hall where the Rogers Brothers got tangled in their suspenders and sprayed each other with their boutonnieres.

Ade's contribution to American literature is in the mainstream of our literary heritage, for he was the benignant observer, the wry philosopher enthroned for his hour upon Poor Richard's cracker barrel. But to seek comic greatness or sustained satiric purpose in Ade is to search among the glitter of a shattered mirror for promise of unity. There is brilliance and sparkle, and here and there a fragment reflects the stars; but it was inescapable that Ade's magnificent scatter of talent should be swept into the dust bin of time.

Little of Ade's work has survived, and though an occasional cackle of delight breaks the stillness when the fables are discovered, it is seldom contagious; for the modern custodians of literary reputation have relegated Ade to the limbo of vernacular raconteurs who misspelled their way through the second half of the nineteenth century. It is unfortunate, for there is much in Ade that remains vital and meaningful today.

Carl Van Doren, who praised Ade highly, said that he was for his time rather than for the ages; but one of Ade's own morals strikes closer to the truth: "It is proper to enjoy the Cheaper Grades of Art, but they should not be formally Indorsed."[8]

George Ade had prepared his own epitaph.

Notes and References

If the source is part of the bibliography, the footnote is listed by author or abbreviated title for clarity. Newspaper reviews of Ade's plays are not cited unless they appeared on a day other than that following the opening performance.

Chapter One

1. Ade, "The Mushy Seventies," p. 73.
2. *Ibid.*, p. 72.
3. "The Dark Ages," p. 82.
4. *Ibid.*, p. 118.
5. *Ibid.*
6. *Ibid.*
7. Kelly, p. 41.
8. *Ibid.*, p. 42.
9. "When I Sowed My Wild Oats," p. 88.
10. John T. McCutcheon, *Drawn from Memory* (Indianapolis, 1950), p. 44.

Chapter Two

1. Kelly, p. 67.
2. Ade's father was a Campbellite; his mother, a Methodist. Despite their attendance at separate churches, they were regular churchgoers, but young Ade's faith was crippled as a consequence of his natural confusion. As a result he became a life-long agnostic.
3. ". . . Keep On Being a Country Boy," p. 56.
4. *Ibid.*
5. "When Good Fellows Got Together," p. 99.
6. Ade was covering the Homestead strike during the Collins beach party and had no part in the obsequies.
7. Isaac Goldberg, *The Theatre of George Jean Nathan* (New York, 1926), p. 59.
8. The eighth series contained eleven articles not written by Ade. A complete history of the series may be found in Dorothy Russo's excellent bibliography.
9. *The Permanent Ade*, pp. 180-84. The story originally appeared in the Chicago *Record*, November 28, 1894.

10. *In Babel*, pp. 49-59. Original appearance: the Chicago *Record*, March 13, 1896.

11. *The Permanent Ade*, p. 199. Original appearance: the Chicago *Record*, July 10, 1897.

12. Kelly, p. 115.

13. *Artie*, p. 131.

14. H. L. Mencken, "The Nature of Slang," in *The Borzoi Reader*, ed. Carl Van Doren (New York, 1936), p. 664.

15. *Artie*, pp. 4-5. Ade soon found it necessary to develop a code of usage, for though he used "slob" in Artie, he later wrote: "There are words of popular circulation, which don't sound well in the mouth or look pretty in type. *Slob* has always been on the *Index Expurgatorius*. Our fellow citizen may be a *dub* or even a *lobster*, and possibly a *mutt*, but let us draw the line on *slob*." "They Simply Wouldn't Let Me Be a High-Brow," *The American Magazine*, XC (December, 1920), 104.

16. *Pink Marsh*, pp. 131-32.

17. *Doc' Horne*, pp. 153-55.

Chapter Three

1. *Fables in Slang*, pp. 147-50.

2. *Ibid.*, p. 9.

3. *Ibid.*, pp. 42-43.

4. *The Girl Proposition*, p. 162.

5. *People You Know*, pp. 23-25.

6. *More Fables*, pp. 242-43.

7. *Ibid.*, pp. 23-35.

8. *Knocking the Neighbors*, p. 3.

9. "They Simply Wouldn't Let Me Be a High-Brow," *op. cit.*, p. 105.

10. *True Bills*, p. 44.

11. *Ibid.*, p. 87.

12. "The Busy, Boiling 90's," p. 156.

13. *Ibid.*

14. The first fable appeared in the Chicago *Record* on September 17, 1897. The last was "The Fable of a Man Who Could Resist Temptation," which appeared in the *Miami Beach Sun* (Winter, 1939).

Chapter Four

1. Unpublished letter in the George Ade Collection at Purdue University.

2. Henry Tyrell, "The College Widow," The New York *World* (September 25, 1904).

3. "George Ade Remembers the Good Old Days. . . ," p. 58.

4. "When 'The Road' Meant Something." An unpublished article, Ade Collection, Purdue.

5. *Single Blessedness and Other Observations*, pp. 64-65.

6. L. Francis Pierce, "George Ade Talks of His Stage Ideals," *The Theatre Magazine*, XLVI (August, 1927), 5.

7. *Ibid.*, p. 288.

8. Unpublished letter to an unidentified professor in California. Dated May 11, 1926, the letter is in the Purdue University Library.

9. Kelly, pp. 162-63.

10. "Victoria—The Night of the Fourth," The New York *Dramatic Mirror* (January 26, 1901), p. 16.

11. The real Sultan of Sulu, Hadji Mohammed Jamulul Kiram, spent most of his life losing money at fan-tan and entertaining his wives, particularly sweet, young Baby. The Sultan lived in a two-room wooden palace on the island of Jolo and wore a soiled red bathrobe and tennis shoes. He got around in a Ford truck. An ineffectual ruler, he soon lost the respect and then the governance of his people, retiring to a life of dalliance with cards, Baby, and cocoanut toddy. Although the Sultan visited the States in 1910, he probably never found out about Ade's play. In 1929 Ade tried to meet the decadent potentate, but an audience was refused. Apparently Ade and McCutcheon had presented the Sultan with a scroll in 1900 which he had been requested to hang in his harem. The scroll read "What is home without a mother." The Sultan once boasted of having a thousand wives at the peak of his interest, but he had no children. At the end of his career he was down to two wives and an annual income, before fan-tan, of $9,000. He abdicated in 1915. See "The Sultan of Sulu Dies; Inspired Comedy by Ade," The New York *Herald Tribune* (June 9, 1936).

12. Unpublished letter, Purdue.

13. "Light Opera Yesterday and To-Day," p. 145.

14. *The Sultan of Sulu* in *The Permanent Ade*, p. 292.

15. For an interesting chapter on the real Sultan of Sulu, see Mc-Cutcheon, *Drawn from Memory, op. cit.*, pp. 142-48. Ade had always been interested in the imperialistic policies of the United States. From July 8 to October 18, 1899, the Chicago *Record* carried a weekly series by Ade entitled "Stories of Benevolent Assimilation."

16. "Light Opera. . . ," p. 145.

17. James S. Metcalfe, "The Drama," *Life*, XLI (January 15, 1903), 54.

18. "Plays and Players," *The Theatre*, III (February, 1903), 34.

19. *Peggy from Paris*, unpublished copyright manuscript in the Library of Congress. A photoduplicate is in the Western Reserve University Library. The passage quoted is on page 12.

Chapter Five

1. "Recalling the Early Tremors of a Timorous Playwright," in the program of The Players 14th Annual Revival of a play important in the history of the theater. In this case *The County Chairman,* produced at the National Theater, New York, during the week of May 25th, 1936.

2. Kelly, p. 177.

3. *The County Chairman,* pp. 7-8. The opening performance of this play was on November 24, 1903, at Wallack's Theater.

4. *Life in Letters of William Dean Howells,* ed. Mildred Howells (New York, 1928), II, 182.

5. James S. Metcalfe, "The Drama," *Life,* XLII (December 11, 1903), 610. For other reviews of Sweatnam's role, see "The Stage," *Munsey's Magazine,* XXXI (July, 1904), 623; and "The Players," *Everybody's Magazine,* X (February, 1904), 248.

6. William Dean Howells, "Some New American Plays," *Harper's Weekly,* XLVIII (January 16, 1904), 88. Howells was not alone in his objections to Ade's pageant. See "Plays and Players," *The Theatre Magazine,* IV (January, 1904), 7.

7. Caspar H. Nannes, *Politics in the American Drama as Revealed by Plays Produced on the New York Stage 1890-1945* (Philadelphia, 1950), p. 31. See also Alan S. Downer, *Fifty Years of American Drama 1900-1950* (Chicago, 1951), p. 118.

8. The program stated: "The scenes of the play are laid in Atwater College, an inland institution of learning lying east of Minnesota and somewhat west of New York."

9. Unpublished letter, Purdue. See also "The First Night." In a letter to Grantland Rice on December 4, 1931, Ade sent Act III in the hope of having Rice include it in an omnibus of sports stories he was preparing. Ade wrote: "This stuff becomes interesting largely from the fact that this play was the first successful play dealing with college life and absolutely the first play on the American stage with football as a central theme. The wise men of the theater said that the public would not be interested in college life or college sport. . . . Remember this, football plays on the talking screen which have been written in the last twenty-five years, every one of them has been a carbon copy of THE COLLEGE WIDOW. It had to be because we used the only workable plot—the player who was fighting against odds and who wins for his team when everything looks dark. No reader should criticize this work until he takes into consideration the fact that this was the first of the football plays and that it deals with the game of 1905. The scene always went big because we played it with two companies—one on stage and one off stage. The large company off stage supplied the songs and yells and worked very carefully on the cues so that the moment the turmoil in the arena quieted down

the talk in front was taken up again. By using this method we got a real effect and maybe it would be interesting to reproduce the whole act" (Unpublished, Purdue Library). Rice published the act in *The Omnibus of Sport* (New York, 1932), pp. 37ff.

10. Unpublished letter, Purdue.

11. "The Stage," *Munsey's Magazine* XXXIII (May, 1905), 204. Ward Morehouse remembered seeing Ty Cobb star in a 1913 tour of the play. High schools usually supplied the football teams for Ade's play, and in Savannah the local school team was engaged for two performances, but stayed for one only—one of the boys was overheard by Cobb when he observed that as an actor Ty was a good ballplayer. Cobb threw them out of the theater, and "Middle-aged stage hands, electricians, carpenters, and bewildered passers-by yanked in from the street, grotesquely attired in football togs, went on that evening in *The College Widow.*" *Matinee Tomorrow: Fifty Years of Our Theater* (New York, 1949), p. 53.

12. *The College Widow*, p. 8.

13. Unpublished letter written in the 1940's, Purdue.

14. A newly established town wanted to be named Georgeade, but Ade requested that it be named after his father. The request was honored as a tribute to the playwright. See Kelly, p. 193.

15. "The College Widow a Phenomenal Success," New York *Dramatic News* (October 1, 1904), p. 17.

16. "America in London," *Punch* (April 29, 1908), p. 322.

17. "Drama," *The Athenaeum* (April 25, 1908), p. 519.

Chapter Six

1. "How I Came to Butt into the Drama," p. 470.

2. *The Sho-Gun*, Act I, p. 7. The play is unpublished. Citations are from the eighty-nine page libretto that Ade filed with the Copyright Office in the Library of Congress. A photoduplicate is in the Western Reserve University Library.

3. James S. Metcalfe, "The Drama," *Life*, XLIV (October 20, 1904), 382-83.

4. "Plays and Players," *The Theatre Magazine*, IV (November, 1904), 270.

5. Kelly, p. 199.

6. Undated manuscript in the Purdue Library. Probably written in the mid-1940's.

7. *The Bad Samaritan*, p. 31. The manuscript of this play is at Purdue; a microfilm copy is available.

8. From Act III. The pagination could not be determined.

9. "The Players," *Everybody's Magazine*, XIII (December, 1905), 809.

10. "The Current Plays," *The Theatre Magazine*, V (October, 1905), 242.

11. *Just Out of College*, pp. 36-37.

12. Copy of an unpublished letter dated October 30, 1905. Purdue University Library.

Chapter Seven

1. *Artie*, Act I, p. 16. The manuscript, unpublished and uncopyrighted, is at Purdue. A photoduplicate is in the John Carroll University Library.

2. Clayton Hamilton, "The Drama," *The Forum*, XXXIX (January, 1908), 371-72. Another critic concurred: "It is hard to persuade a person to like a youth whose only bid for popularity is made up of impertinence, bad English, unlimited nerve and disregard for veracity. He was not a bad sort of fellow in book form, but in the form of stage representation one is seized with a strong desire to spank him." "Reviews of New Plays," The New York *Dramatic Mirror*, LVIII (November 9, 1907), 3.

3. *Father and the Boys*, p. 7.

4. James S. Metcalfe, "The Drama," *Life*, LI (March 19, 1908), 300.

5. *The Fair Co-Ed*, Act I, p. 16. A photoduplicate of the libretto in the Copyright Office, Washington, D. C. is in the Western Reserve University Library.

6. Channing Pollock, "Spring Fever and the Theaters," *The Smart Set*, XXVII (April, 1909), 152. Music for the play was written by Lester H. Lipinsky, George Ade Davis, and Harold A. Lipinsky.

7. Kelly, p. 201.

8. George Jean Nathan, "The Dramas of the Fore and Aft," *The Smart Set*, XXX (March, 1910), 151.

9. *The City Chap*, Act III, p. 18. The manuscript of this unpublished play is at Purdue. A photoduplicate is in the John Carroll University Library.

10. *U.S. Minister Bedloe*, Act I, p. 19. Unpublished and uncopyrighted, the only known copy of the play is a prompter's copy which I found in the theater collection of the New York Public Library. A photoduplicate is in the John Carroll University Library.

11. Kelly, 201.

12. Luther B. Anthony, "Technical Tendencies," *The Dramatist*, II (April, 1911), 147-48.

13. "When the Road Meant Something," unpublished, unpaginated manuscript at Purdue. Ade's financial success was the envy of his literary friends. In an unpublished letter to Ade dated July 24, 1917, Finley Peter Dunne wrote: "I think of you always with unmixed envy, and wonder how anyone could be so rich who has done so little." Purdue. Brand Whitlock wrote to Clarence Darrow: "Last night

George Ade was here to see the production of his new play, 'Father and the Boys' with William H. Crane in the title role, and as I sat with him in the box and thought of the old days when we were poor reporters in Chicago and of all that has happened since, and reflected on how hard we had both worked, and looked at him sitting there with all the money he has made for himself, and then looked at me with all the money I have not made for myself, I wondered if, after all, it is worth while or not—but then I must not say that for, of course it is worth while . . ." *The Letters of Brand Whitlock*, ed. Allan Nevins (New York, 1936), p. 85.

14. "The Hardest $100,000 That I Ever Earned," p. 134.

15. "The First Night," p. 18.

16. Ade made direct or indirect contributions to at least fourteen motion pictures.

Chapter Eight

1. Kelly, p. 160.

2. "The Hardest $100,000 That I Ever Earned," p. 132.

3. The unpaginated, unpublished manuscript is at Purdue. A photoduplicate is in the John Carroll University Library.

4. Clayton Hamilton, "The Drama," *The Forum*, XL (November, 1908), 441.

5. "At the Playhouse," *The Theatre Magazine*, VIII (November, 1908), xiiiff.

6. Unpublished letter from Flo Irwin to Ade, dated September 17, 1927. Purdue.

7. *Il Janitoro* in *Midland Humor*, ed. Jack Conroy (New York, 1947), pp. 150-53. Although *The Back-Stair Investigation* was the first Ade play produced, *Il Janitoro* appeared in the Chicago *Record* on April 2, 1896.

8. A photoduplicate of this unpublished manuscript has been made from the copyright manuscript in the Library of Congress. It is in the Western Reserve University Library.

9. Anna Morgan, *My Chicago* (Chicago, 1918), p. 193.

10. *Marse Covington* in *The Permanent Ade*, p. 273.

11. *The Mayor and the Manicure* in *One Act Plays for Stage and Study* (New York, 1925), pp. 33-34.

12. *Nettie*, pp. 13-15.

13. *Aunt Fanny from Chautauqua* in *One Act Plays for Stage and Study* (New York, 1949), p. 15.

14. "The Persecuted Wife," p. 6.

15. "The Willing Performer," p. 13. This play is a dramatization of "The Fable of the Two Mandolin Players and the Willing Performer," the most frequently reprinted of Ade's fables. Its initial appearance was in the Chicago *Record*, October 7, 1899; it was later included in *Fables in Slang*.

Chapter Nine

1. *In Pastures New*, p. 187.

2. Grant C. Knight, "The Pastry Period in Literature," *Saturday Review of Literature*, XXVII (December 16, 1944), 5. See also Carl Van Doren, *The American Novel* (New York, 1946), p. 217.

3. *The Slim Princess*, p. 7.

4. Ade's last script, never produced, was to star Will Rogers who had portrayed Jim Hackler in the motion picture version of *The County Chairman*. Of the latter play Ade wrote to James R. Rathbun: "They have changed it a good deal, putting it in Wyoming instead of Indiana and introducing a lot of new story stuff, but they have kept many of the old names and in the scenes that are essential to the drama they have used a lot of my old talk including many of the speeches which are quoted by the critics. The public seems to like the play and I suppose it will do me no harm, even though I can hardly claim it as my own." Unpublished letter dated January 29, 1935, Purdue. Will Rogers' death ended what promised to be a mutually profitable association with Ade.

5. Selections from this book appear in *The Permanent Ade* and *The America of George Ade*.

6. *The Old-Time Saloon*, p. 26. For a study of Ade's social criticism, see Balfour R. Daniels, "George Ade as Social Critic," *Mississippi Quarterly*, XII (Fall, 1959), 194-204.

7. Kelly, p. 236. Ade's voluminous correspondence evidences a genuine interest in people and their problems. He was a soft touch for the down-and-out and invariably proved helpful to those making serious requests. Max Eastman asked Ade for a few lines on Bergson's theory of humor. Six days later on May 11, 1936, Ade replied: "You have asked me a question which is hard to answer. I suspect that Bergson was nearly right when he said that all laughter at the expense of someone else is really founded on a 'feeling of superiority,' on the part of the amused person over the victim of the incident which arouses the laughter. However, a great deal of the laughter caused by stage performances and public addresses may depend upon the surprise element—the unexpected statement of some fact illustrating some vanity or foible or weakness of human nature. Maybe this all goes right back to the feeling of superiority. I fear that too many of us enjoy seeing our fellow creatures make stupid mistakes or involve themselves in embarrassing situations or saying the wrong thing at the right time and we are impelled to laugh at them. However, it may often happen that laughter will be aroused by the statement of an obvious or well-known fact in an entirely new way." Published in part in Max Eastman, *The Enjoyment of Laughter* (New York, 1948), p. 335. Eastman edited out the section on "the surprise element" in humor.

Shortly after answering Eastman's query, Cyril Clemens asked Ade for a definition of humor. The reply: "You have given me some assignment when you asked me to define humor. I know that it is not what a great many people think it is—jokes, wise cracks and puns. Humor is the reflection of a mood. It is the revelation of some individual's point of view which enables him to discover the ridiculous, the unusual or the silly in man of the standard human performances. Mark Twain had it in an abundant degree. Among present day writers who have something of the same knack may be mentioned P. G. Wodehouse, Harry Leon Wilson and Damon Runyan. A man gifted with humor does not indulge in jokes or attempt to be comical but reveals, by subtle methods, some of the frailties of human nature. This is about as near as I can come to describing the darn thing." Unpublished letter dated November 28, 1937. Both letters are in the Purdue University Library.

8. *People You Know*, p. 25.

Selected Bibliography

PRIMARY SOURCES

Bibliographically, George Ade is splendidly preserved in a handsome volume: Dorothy Ritter Russo, *A Bibliography of George Ade, 1866-1944* (Indianapolis: Indiana Historical Society, 1947).

A. *Autobiography*

"The Busy, Boiling 90's," *Hearst's International Magazine*, LXXXI (November, 1926), 76ff.

"The Dark Ages," *Hearst's International Magazine*, LXXXI (August, 1926), 82ff.

"The First Night," *Colliers*, XXXVII (June 16, 1906), 17-18.

"For the First Time in My Life I'm Going to Talk about Myself," *Hearst's International Magazine*, LXXVIII (June, 1925), 102ff.

"George Ade Remembers the Good Old Days When One Might Have a Big Night for 45 Cents," *Hearst's International Magazine*, LXXIX (October, 1925), 58ff.

"The Hardest $100,000 That I Ever Earned," *Hearst's International Magazine*, LXXIX (November, 1925), 58ff.

"How I Came to Butt into the Drama," *Pearson's Magazine*, XII (November, 1904), 468-71.

"How to Live in the Country," *Hearst's International Magazine*, LXXX (January, 1926), 56ff.

"I Keep Myself Young by Doing Twice as Much Work as I Did 20 Years Ago," *Hearst's International Magazine*, LXXX (February, 1926), 76ff.

"I Knew Them When—" *Hearst's International Magazine*, LXXXI (December, 1926), 74ff.

"Log Cabin Days," *Hearst's International Magazine*, LXXX (April, 1926), 82ff.

"The Mushy Seventies," *Hearst's International Magazine*, LXXXI (September, 1926), 72ff.

"My Mother and Father," *Hearst's International Magazine*, LXXX (March, 1926), 80ff.

"Remember Me as the Man Who Might Have Bunked with John L.," *Hearst's International Magazine*, LXXLX (September, 1925), 66ff.

"Soft Hats, High Hats, and Coronets," *Hearst's International Magazine*, LXXIX (July, 1925), 44ff.

"Some High Spots," *Hearst's International Magazine,* LXXIX (August, 1925), 66ff.
"To Get Along, Keep on Being a Country Boy," *Hearst's International Magazine,* LXXIX (December, 1925), 56ff.
"When Good Fellows Got Together," *Hearst's International Magazine,* LXXXII (February, 1927), 98ff.
"When I Sowed My Wild Oats," *Hearst's International Magazine,* LXXXI (October, 1926), 88ff.

B. *Fables and Essays*

Ade's Fables. New York: Doubleday, Page & Co., 1914.
Artie. Chicago: Herbert S. Stone & Co., 1896.
Bang! Bang! New York: J. H. Sears & Co., 1928.
Breaking into Society. New York: Harper & Brothers, 1904.
Doc' Horne. Chicago: Herbert S. Stone & Co., 1899.
Fables in Slang. Chicago: Herbert S. Stone & Co., 1900.
Forty Modern Fables. New York: R. H. Russell, 1901.
The Girl Proposition. New York: R. H. Russell, 1902.
Hand-Made Fables. New York: Doubleday, Page & Co., 1920.
In Babel. New York: McClure, Phillips & Co., 1903.
In Pastures New. New York: McClure, Phillips & Co., 1906.
Knocking the Neighbors. New York: Doubleday, Page & Co., 1912.
More Fables. Chicago: Herbert S. Stone & Co., 1900.
People You Know. New York: R. H. Russell, 1903.
Pink Marsh. Chicago: Herbert S. Stone & Co., 1897.
Single Blessedness and Other Observations. New York: Doubleday, Page & Co., 1922.
Stories of the Streets and of the Town, ed. Franklin J. Meine. Chicago: The Caxton Club, 1941.
True Bills. New York: Harper & Brothers, 1904.

C. *Plays*

The College Widow. New York: Samuel French, 1924.
The County Chairman. New York: Samuel French, 1924.
Father and the Boys. New York: Samuel French, 1924.
Just Out of College. New York: Samuel French, 1924.
"Light Opera Yesterday and To-day," *The Theatre Magazine,* III (June, 1903), 145.
The Mayor and the Manicure. New York: Samuel French, 1923.
Nettie. New York: Samuel French, 1923.
"The Perfect Play Is One Which Entertains the Audience without Poisoning It," *The Theatre Magazine,* XLVI (August, 1927), 5.
"The Persecuted Wife," *Liberty,* II (July 4, 1925), 6-10.
Speaking to Father. New York: Samuel French, 1923.
"The Willing Performer," *The Country Gentleman* (February, 1928), 12ff.

D. *Miscellaneous Works*

The Old-Time Saloon. New York: Ray Long & Richard Smith, 1931.
One Afternoon with Mark Twain. Chicago: The Mark Twain Society of Chicago, 1939.
The Slim Princess. Indianapolis: Bobbs-Merrill, 1907.
Verses and Jingles. Indianapolis: Bobbs-Merrill, 1911.

E. *Anthologies*

The America of George Ade, ed. Jean Shepherd. New York: Putnam, 1960.
Thirty Fables in Slang. New York: Arrow Editions, 1933.
The Permanent Ade, ed. Fred C. Kelly. Indianapolis: Bobbs-Merrill, 1947.

SECONDARY SOURCES

A. *Biography*

KELLY, FRED C. *George Ade: Warmhearted Satirist.* Indianapolis: Bobbs-Merrill, 1947. Although adulatory and uncritical, it is the only full-length biography and is therefore indispensable. The book is built upon extensive quotation from interviews and upon the uncollected autobiographical articles. It is not annotated.
MATSON, LOWELL. "Ade: Who Needed None," *The Literary Review,* V (Autumn, 1961), 99-114. The best short biographical sketch and general survey of Ade's career.

B. *Criticism*

BAUERLE, R. F. "A Look at the Language of George Ade," *American Speech,* XXXIII (February, 1958), 77-79. A cursory glance at Ade's slang.
CARGILL, OSCAR. *Intellectual America.* New York: Macmillan, 1941. Ade is one of the last of the purely indigenous humorists. The fables "are 'revolt from the village' and nothing more."
CLARK, JOHN ABBOTT. "Ade's Fables in Slang: An Appreciation," *South Atlantic Quarterly,* XLVI (October, 1947), 537-44. A colorful rant on the stupidity of the critics, the joys of the fables, the delights of Ade's language, Ade's social criticism, and Ade's "basic American . . . vividly ageless in the matter of epithet and idiom."
DICKINSON, T. H. *Playwrights of the New American Theatre.* New York: Macmillan, 1925. High praise for Ade's plays, which are "milestones in the history of our native drama." The fables, "for insight into character and pungency of expression take their place with the best work of the 'character writers' of the past."

Selected Bibliography

DUFFY, BERNARD. *The Chicago Renaissance in American Letters.* Lansing, Michigan: Michigan State College Press, 1954. Sloughs off Ade as a "master gag-writer" lost in "the blind alley of routine entertainment." Dismisses the fables and their language as superficial. Provocative.

EVANS, BERGEN. "George Ade, Rustic Humorist," *American Mercury,* LXX (March, 1950), 321-29. An eloquent analysis of the fables and their popularity. Sees the fables as impudent travesties of McGuffey's Readers.

HOWELLS, WILLIAM DEAN. "Certain of the Chicago School of Fiction," *North American Review,* CLXXVI (May, 1903), 734-46. Applauds Ade's lack of literary pose and considers him the embodiment of the American spirit "speaking one slang, living one life, meaning one thing."

––––––. "Editor's Easy Chair," *Harper's Monthly,* CXXXIV (February, 1917), 442-45. Contains an appreciation of *In Babel* and places Ade in the tradition of American humor.

MASSON, THOMAS. *Our American Humorists.* New York: Moffat, Yard & Co., 1922. Laudatory survey of Ade's life and work. Finds the fables "concentrated food; to be taken as a tonic, say one or two after a meal."

MAYORGA, MARGARET G. *A Short History of the American Drama.* New York: Dodd, Mead & Co., 1932. Contains a brief survey of Ade's principal plays and finds him "very definitely influenced by Hoyt."

MENCKEN, H. L. *Prejudices: First Series.* New York: A. A. Knopf, 1919. An enthusiastic appraisal that finds Ade to be a genuine literary craftsman who "deserves a respectable place in the second rank."

PATTEE, FRED LEWIS. *The New American Literature.* New York: Century, 1930. A sensitive discussion of Ade's humor in which there is "an element that is more than mere buffoonery." Some of the fables, and "to some extent the comedies, seem destined to survive—at least for a time."

QUINN, ARTHUR HOBSON. *A History of the American Drama from the Civil War to the Present Day.* Vol. II. New York: F. S. Crofts & Co., 1937. Places Ade in the mainstream of American dramatic achievement: "From the two Jonathans in *The Contrast* and *The Forest Rose,* through the work of Harrigan and Hoyt, the tradition passed on unbroken to George Ade and George Cohan."

VAN DOREN, CARL. "Old Wisdom in a New Tongue," *The Century,* CV (January, 1923), 471-80. Vies with Mencken's essay as the finest on the subject. Ade is "a satirist of genius," who "belongs so unquestionably to his folk that he has a license to ridicule it."

Index

Index